PRAISE FOR T

CW01653522

This book is a great resource featuring 50 prope successfully doing what you may want to do, shari to help you create your personal and business fo experts in response to beginners' questions, giving your desired life.

Andrew Batt, Multiple business owner & CEO of World Game Changers CIC

The quickest way into property, or any business you want to get into, is go and find somebody doing what you're doing and going off to work with them for free... this is what this book offers.

Harvey, Founder of "Growth Properties" group

This is the property beginner's Bible.

Paul Percival, Director of Luma Properties Ltd & Java Properties Ltd (based in South Wales)

A one-stop invaluable resource for newbie property investors to find out everything they need to know in order to successfully get started in property. It's a great platform for people to draw off other people's experiences, skills, wisdom and knowledge to navigate their own best way.

Hazel de Kloe, Multi-million-pound property portfolio holder; award-winning co-founder of coaching and mentoring business 'Why Property Works' and 'The Freedom Club'

This book will help people who are willing to be helped. When people who have done this stuff for 30 years and made all the mistakes so you don't have to, do me a favour. Do the hard yards with their advice. Don't forget it because that advice was probably learned the hard way by someone willing to share it philanthropically so that you don't have to.

Paul Million, Landlord and Property Developer for over 30 years

The book will be wonderful for anyone starting out on their property journey. I wish I'd read something similar when I was starting out. I think the collaboration of 50 people sharing their perspectives is amazing.

Michelle Walker-Smith, Award-winning founder of Aqua Lettings Ltd & Michelle Walker Smith Coaching

A great book for beginners who want to get the real behind-the-scenes view of property investing from people who have been there and got the t-shirt.

Jeannette Linfoot, Property investor, business advisor, mentor & host of the Brave, Bold, Brilliant podcast

PROPERTY INVESTING BEGINNER'S MASTERMIND SERIES

Vol 1

The 1st Place.

What is the best learning, education and training for me?

Alex Sapala & Sharon Griffiths

First published in Great Britain 2023 by Alex Sapala and Sharon Griffiths

Text Copyright © Alex Sapala and Sharon Griffiths

All rights reserved. No parts of this publication may be reproduced, stored in a retrieval system, or transmitted in any form or by any means, electronic, mechanical, photocopying, recording or otherwise, without prior written permission from the publisher.

British Library Cataloguing in Publication Data
A CIP catalogue record for this book is available upon request from the British Library

ISBN: 978-1-8383506-1-1

Alex Sapala and Sharon Griffiths have asserted their right under the Copyright, Design and Patents Act 1988 to be identified as the authors of this work

Other titles in the series coming soon:
Getting Started
Do all my Ducks Need to be in a Row?
The Challenge of Me
My Power Team

ABOUT THE AUTHORS

Alex Sapala

Alex is a UK-based family man turned prolific property investor and developer, specialising in NMLI (No Money Left In) strategies including HMOs, semi-commercial and commercial conversions and BTLs. As an award-winning chartered accountant and author of The No.1 Amazon bestseller, *The Business Path to Wealth Creation*, he shares business and financial information as well as capturing people's inspirational stories through his 'Business, Wealth and Mindset' podcast. He is an accomplished investment banker with experience from some of the world's renowned financial institutions, including The Royal Bank of Scotland (RBS), Deloitte and JP Morgan. Alex is also a mentor, coach, trainer and founder of Elite Edge Wealth Academy and is passionate about mindset, knowledge sharing and financial empowerment.

Sharon Griffiths

Sharon started to learn how to invest in property in 2017 and has built up a buy-to-let portfolio with her husband which, along with her pension, has enabled her to fund her chosen lifestyle. She is a Director of World Game Changers CIC and is a published author, trained life coach and experienced educational professional, having worked in the educational sector for over 30 years in a range of roles, including teaching, training and management, while also raising her two daughters who were born in the late 1990s.

ACKNOWLEDGEMENTS

From Alex

To my co-creator Sharon Griffiths, tireless and meticulous in curiosity and always striving for perfection – I have learnt a lot from you! To Pamela Naphiyo for her inspiration and encouragement, and the team at Elite Edge Wealth Academy.

From Sharon

Thank you to Tim, Megan and Âine, my reason for being; and to Mum and Dad, who are no longer on earth, but never gave up on me; and everyone who has been invaluable in the collaborative co-creation of this book.

From Alex and Sharon

To the meticulous and patient Lisa Mackerness who painstakingly transcribed every interview, and to the amazing Becky Miles for all the expert editorial work. To the inspirational and creative Rebecca Wheele who worked with us to design the book covers and create our website, and to Felix Pour Joseph for the amazing funnel and promotion work. To all of the contributors for selflessly sharing their knowledge, experiences and wisdom, offering priceless value for the benefit of us all. And finally to you aspiring wealth builders out there – whatever your background, whatever your field to date, whatever your walk of life – your journey of a thousand steps will begin with The 1st Place! Here's to your success!

CONTENTS

INTRODUCTION

by Sharon Griffiths

In his book, *Start with Why*, Simon Sinek writes, 'If we are starting with the wrong questions, if we don't understand the cause, then even the right answers will steer us wrong ... eventually. The truth, you see, is always revealed ... eventually.'

And so, this is where we start with this two-volume set of books; with authentic, honest questions asked by curious people, beginners in their property investing career or, like myself and Alex, people on a curious adventure.

The questions shared in these books have been asked by curious property investors in the early stages of their investing journey, and have been answered by 50 experts in the property business. The people asking the questions weren't too worried about whether the questions were right or wrong, but they wanted answers that that would help them do what they want to do and create the future they want to live, on their terms.

Curiosity is the foundation of these books. They provide a great opportunity for collaborative creation, working with others who are successful in what they do, and were borne out of The Curiosity Club, our room where we hosted meetings on the audio social-media platform Clubhouse during May and June 2021. The discussions held there prompted us to arrange the questions into book form, and to ask 50 expert contributors to share their knowledge and give us their answers to these questions.

I remember so clearly when I said to Alex, 'I've got all these questions asked by beginners in our Clubhouse room, and they could be of help to more people in the future. They are wasted hidden on the pages of my notebook. Do you want to write a book?' Alex said 'YES', and we both agreed on this aligned aim, to write a book that will help others who are in similar positions to those we were in when we started to invest in property. We soon realised we had enough material for two books! Readers can take from them what they choose and when, so they can reduce fear of the unknown future and increase potential opportunities for success, as defined by them, in whatever they wish to do.

We are living in an unprecedented period of change, where all around us many people are living with fear and uncertainty about their future. Our aim was to intentionally and purposefully create a collaborative project that,

- helps reduce fear and doubt
- increases knowledge based on hindsight and foresight
- creates more certainty, positivity and hope when faced with personal challenges
- provides information that enables and inspires people to take their next steps with more confidence
- allows readers to see the potential for opportunities and personal transformation
- is beneficial for those that work with us

Additionally, we aim to contribute to the health, wellbeing, certainty, wealth and positive feelings people may feel, desire and create, not just in their immediate future, but also for their legacy and future generations.

Who is this book for?

- Those who have just started out in property investing
- Those who are curious about how to become a successful property investor
- Curious people who want to become more successful at what they do
- Curious people who want more certainty so they can act with more foresight and with the benefit of hindsight

This book contains interviews with 50 successful property investors, who each followed the same process and answered the same 24 questions between October 2021 to March 2022. This book – Volume 1 in the series – contains their answers to the first 11 of these questions, while Volume 2 contains their answers to questions 12–24. Alex and I have gotten to know each contributor over many years though what we do and in our various networks, and the words shared in this book are their truths, their thoughts, based on what has enabled them to be successful at what they do. Each person holds life-long learning as one of their highest values, and has invested in themselves for many years. They understand the significance and importance of goal-setting and purpose, and each has built one or more businesses based on achieving their aims. They have generously shared their knowledge and speak from their personal experiences (both successes and failures), with the aim that readers can create their own future plans based on the answers given.

My story

I have been curious for as long as I can remember, I always wanted to find out answers to questions in those subjects I was curious about until I was satisfied and could move on to the next thing I wanted to do. My inherent inquisitiveness led me to creating experiences, learning from my own experiences, and those of others. Before the internet came along, I used to read newspapers, books written by experts, encyclopaedias and magazines endlessly.

I asked questions to anyone I could find who would provide answers that would satisfy me. Over time, I learnt that those who were successful at what they were doing were the ones who would provide answers that satisfied my curiosity. As a seeker of knowledge, much of my childhood resources of time and money were invested in paying for transport to libraries and buying resources I could afford. Presents usually consisted of books and encyclopaedias. My head was always in a book, and if my curiosity wasn't satisfied, I would seek out new resources and people to answer my questions.

At 17, my dad said to me, with exasperation, 'Why do you ask so many questions?', to which my mum replied, 'Because she takes after you, that's why!'

I built a career in the education sector for over 30 years from the 1980s. My curiosity enabled and created opportunities for me to experience a wide range of work roles, as well as being an inspired and enthusiastic lifelong learner.

My jobs fed my ongoing personal and professional development and included being a judo coach, a teacher, tutor, trainer, a careers advisor, a team leader, a health and safety risk assessor, a curriculum manager and a reflexologist and massage practitioner with my own business. I built my wealth on my unforgiving curiosity and have created a varied, fulfilling and meaningful life with many curious adventures and numerous new beginnings.

I imagine that I will forever be curious about what is of interest to me or what I think may be of interest to those I have helped or may help.

My mission is to bespokely connect people to opportunities and my vision is that of connecting curious people worldwide so that they are inspired and empowered to create their own 'Shappiness' – an intentional state of success and happiness.

I hope that this collaboratively created book, the first in our Property Investing Beginner's Mastermind series, goes towards achieving my vision as I live in mission co-creating it with my co-author Alex Sapala and each person who has contributed to it.

Curious questions

From my experience of thousands of children, personally and professionally, curiosity appears to be a natural human trait and with it we can begin to learn more about ourselves, our interests and the world around us. We can also explore and identify our choices and options as part of a decision-making process. We ask questions from childhood, with a definite purpose of discovering answers, and it is around the age of two when our first questions happen and begin with these singular words:

Why? How? When? Who? What?

These monosyllabic words start questions off, enabling us to discover and gain greater understanding of the world in our head and outside.

As we develop our questioning skills, communicate and connect with ourselves and others, we learn to develop the length of our sentences and questions in order to meet that first basic human need of certainty and the second human need of variety (or uncertainty).

Curiosity as a tool enables us to then progress to learning and exploring new things that come into our life through connection with others. As we step outside our comfort zones, and then as we begin to help and serve others, we can increasingly and more skilfully develop our questioning skills to identify how we cannot just meet our needs, but also meet the needs of others we may encounter in our lives, so helping them along the way.

I love this poem by Allan Ahlberg. Anyone who remembers being a young child at school may relate to it. I first read it, when I was training to be a secondary school Geography teacher in 1983 and I have regularly read it since; it makes me smile to myself. It resonated greatly with me in terms of what I'd experienced though my life up to that point and it still does now, at age 60, as I write this book with Alex and all the contributors.

THE 1ST PLACE.

Please Mrs Butler

Please Mrs Butler
This boy Derek Drew
Keeps copying my work, Miss.
What shall I do?

Go sit in the hall, dear.
Go and sit in the sink.
Take your books on the roof, my lamb.
Do whatever you think

Please Mrs Butler
This boy Derek Drew
Keeps taking my rubber, Miss.
What shall I do?

Keep it in your hand dear
Hide it up your vest
Swallow it if you like, love.
Do what you think best

Please Mrs Butler
This boy Derek Drew
Keeps calling me rude names, Miss.
What shall I do?

Lock yourself in the cupboard, dear.
Run away to sea.
Do whatever you can, my flower.
But don't ask me!

Allan Ahlberg

The Curiosity Club

Our constant need to ask questions is one reason why, in The Curiosity Club, we created a series of eight rooms over eight weeks between May and June 2021. We wanted to create a safe space where beginners could ask any questions on stage, to experts who answered them. Over that time, more than 120 questions were asked on the theme of 'Property Mastermind'. No question was considered stupid and we could begin to enable those asking them to go through the four stages of their individual learning process, as we all do:

- Unconsciously incompetent
- Consciously incompetent
- Consciously competent
- Unconsciously competent

About this book

Alex and Sharon started in the teaching and coaching industry from a place of wanting to help others to become better equipped in their roles, to both help themselves and, in turn, other people. In doing so, they have encountered many inspiring and knowledgeable people who use their skills to continually improve what they do. This book aims to do the same; to help you learn how to invest in property successfully, and keep improving what you do. And it does this by sharing answers to 11 key beginner's questions from 50 successful property investors.

By reading and implementing the information and wisdom shared, you will be able to

- Create your own success
- Unlock many secrets to conjuring a successful business mindset of a property investor
- Turn your knowledge into property income
- Create the impact you deserve without being stuck working in a job you may not wish to be in, dependant on that one main stream of income

Tried-and-tested resources and strategies are shared within these two covers by people who have faced and overcome obstacles and, despite many challenges, have successfully worked towards making 'it' happen. And what is 'it'?

'It' is the life that each contributor has defined, created and carved out for themselves, just as they envisioned it to be. And they did not do this alone, but alongside others in their networks who are on the same path.

This book is a great starting point; in fact, it is The 1st Place for you if you,

- Want an easy place from which to start learning and identify what you may want to do
- Want to experience and achieve more success
- Want to start learning about property investing
- Want to short cut your way to success, through strategies and tactics shared by successful experts
- Are curious about how to become successful in property Investing, but know that you don't have to do things on your own
- Have started to learn about how to invest, but are feeling a little overwhelmed
- Have questions that you feel may be silly or too simple or just appear to be obvious, but DON'T know the answers to
- Want more certainty about the future
- Want to save money, time, energy and potentially prolonged negative stress
- Want to create more of what you want in your life
- Want to overcome the feelings of overwhelm, procrastination and state of 'analysis paralysis' you may be feeling
- Want to know who to ask your questions to and what to ask them

THE 1ST PLACE.

- Want to know where to learn and the best way to learn
- Wonder how to navigate your way through all the information out there to find what YOU need

It features interviews with successful property investors, each answering the same questions asked by property beginners around the subject of 'what is the best learning, education and training for me?'

Each investor kindly gave their time, knowledge and wisdom freely in order to achieve their desired goal of helping others. They each bought into and aligned with the vision of the book, and gave their answers free of charge. They didn't know which questions they would be asked when interviewed, so did not have time to pre-prepare their answers. As a result, they each replied in a completely unfiltered, raw and authentic way.

We hope that when you read the variety of answers given, you are able to step into the new space that you are creating and choreographing without fear, knowing that there may be a little more certainty for you ahead. And that with this certainty, it is possible that your confidence may increase, because you aren't facing your future alone – there are many who are there wanting to help you create more certainty and be more creative as you step into a new unknown world, towards where you want to be.

And finally, I remember as a child, my dad and one of my grandmas used to say to me, 'Don't ever forget where you came from.' In the case of this book, both Alex and I shall never forget where both ourselves and this book came from. We have gratitude for its source of inspiration and for what it may give in the future, in terms of inspiring and enabling readers to move forward with more self-confidence with what they choose to do, how they do choose to do it and for their chosen reasons why. As Alex would say, 'In the end it truly is down to you, but it isn't all about you.'

The Contributors

We would like to thank all contributors listed below for giving their time to share their unique and individual learnings, knowledge and golden nuggets of wisdom in order to achieve the overall desired goal of helping others. Each one knows and acknowledges that:

They have gratitude for where they are now and what went before

They openly acknowledge they would not be in their present position if it was not for the support, help, and guidance and accountability they had received along their own journey in property investing and in life itself.

They want to share and help others in an empathic professional way

They know that what they share is of great value to the reader, not just within the world of business but also in life. Each person has lived a life, invested in themselves, learnt about how to successfully be what they want to become, made and owned their decisions, faced and overcome their own personal challenges and has a story to tell. And through their experiences and learnings, they can say what they feel is relevant, because it is highly likely they once asked the same or similar questions when they needed help as beginners or even after some experience or others have asked them the same or similar questions.

The contributors are

Adam Huzzey
Alex Sapala
Andrew Batt
Caroline Borg
Craig Phillips
Darren Burrows
Darren Grigas
Dave Goodfellow
David Bennett
Debbie Sheriff
Elizabeth Baitson
Emerald Fisk
Fiona Crossley
Halstead Ottley
Harvey Natalie Bailey
Natasha Collins
Paul Duval
James Doran
Jamie Madill
Jane Bayler
Jeanette Linfoot
Jez Wood
John Foster
John Philbin
Julie Hogbin
Kevin Poneskis
Kim Hendle
Lorraine Harris
Michelle Walker Smith
Motiul Islam
Muzzie Nduna
Victor Lupu
Vito Ianelli
Paul Million
Paul Percival
Paul Tinker
Paula Bushnell
Peter Wood
Ranjit Seehra
Richard Stone
Rick Cusimano
Rochelle Gilburn
Sarah Harding
Sharon Griffiths
Shaz Nawaz
Stephanie Taylor
Tony Harding
Hazel de Kloe
Jack Dawhra

And the questions are:

Volume 1

How do I choose the right education, training and learning for me?

What happens when I start learning and realise there's more I don't know than I do know, or that there's too much to learn?

How can I use my thoughts to help me do what I want?

How do I know which people to connect with to help me?

Is free help real help for me?

How shall I prepare for opportunities?

Which beginners' property books would you recommend?

Which property strategy should I follow?

THE 1ST PLACE.

How do I get the properties I want?

What kind of money do I need to get my first property?

How can I find people I can trust to give me the right guidance?

Volume 2

What are the best courses to go on?

How do I know what to say yes to?

What do I do next?

What type of networking events should I go to?

What shall I say at networking events?

I want to leave my job. How can I use property investment to do this?

At what point do I leave my job to go into property investing?

How do I work out WHAT I want, WHY I want it, WHERE to get it and WHEN to visit?

How do I choose my property strategy?

How do I choose my property area?

Deal sourcing – what's the best way to learn it?

And how much will that cost?

How do I gain experience in property investing when I don't know very much and haven't got any properties?

Let's make a start with the first contributor and see what they have to say...

Disclaimer:

Each interviewee provided their own thoughts based on their knowledge, experience, expertise. They were not informed of questions prior to interview, nor of the identity any of the other interviewees. Almost all of them have chosen to answer every single question, but occasionally they have chosen NOT to answer a specific question for their own reasons.

If you choose to explore any information, advice or guidance in this book, it is important that you undertake your own due diligence in order to make well-informed choices.

THE INTERVIEWS

1. Adam Huzzey

About Adam

Adam is an entrepreneur focusing on property and wealth management. He is a multiple business and property owner with businesses specialising in wealth creation and asset acquisitions. Adam has extensive experience in property, focusing on HMO, BTL and commercial conversions, and he helps to create everlasting hands-off wealth for business partners through property. A mindset public speaker, Adam excels in relationship building and motivational leadership. His specialties are: Property Investments, Financial Investments, Mindset, Business relationships.

Based	Berkshire
Investment location	Nationwide
Strategies	Commercial / Conversion, BTL, HMO, SA
Favourite sayings/ affirmations/mottos	Organisation is the key to happiness
Three key learnings you would like to share with readers	• Time is always running out • Take action, NOW! • Hold no regrets

Job (if in a job previously)

Managing partner for the Domo group.

Why did you leave your job?

Because I could.

What do you love about your life now?

Freedom / the ability to give back and help others.

Education, training, learning

- Mainly from Progressive Property
- Regular masterminds
- Making mistakes

Favourite books

- Robert T. Kiyosaki, *Rich Dad Poor Dad*
- Mark Manson, *The Subtle Art of Not Giving a F*ck*
- Rob Moore, *Money*

Contact details

Website: www.domodevelopments.com
Email: adam@domo-group.net
Mobile: 07999 599952

Adam's Answers

How do I choose the right education, training and learning for me?

With difficulty. I think a lot of the more superior training companies will offer free days where it doesn't cost you any money. You can go around, you can dive in, meet mentors, meet people, meet delegates, and I think if you are unsure of what company to choose, then you should take advantage of those free days and see which one resonates with you the most and then make a common-sense decision based on that.

What happens when I start learning and realise there's more I don't know than I do know, or that there's too much to learn?

Be grateful. There is stuff you don't know. Everyone is always learning, constantly. We're all still learning. There are things now that I can't believe I didn't know, or don't know, but I'm excited to know and I'm excited to learn. I think the realisation that you don't know everything and that you certainly won't is quite humbling. So, I would say embrace it, enjoy it and learn.

How can I use my thoughts to help me do what I want?

Make sure they don't stay as thoughts. Make sure they become reality and you put them into action. A lot of people have all these wonderful ideas and they jot them all down, but then don't actually take the step to put them into reality. So, as long as they turn from thoughts to action very quickly, I think you'll be ok.

How do I know which people to connect with to help me?

I would start by looking at people that are active and on display on social media. It's not to say that everyone on display or quite frequently posts or whatever are going to be at that high level you want them to be at, but I think it's a great place to start.

Networking is massively important. I think if you go to enough networking events or you do enough socialising within the property circle you like, the same names are going to crop up. You are going to get to know the same names and people and identify with them a bit more.

You will have to do a bit of research, but if you are just going to do that from your laptop all the time it's not going to help. You need to get out, get involved in networking on a 1-2-1 basis and in groups, go to various events and then take it from there.

Is free help real help for me?

Yes, totally. There are many, many, many bits of free advice that we've be given, or I've be given, over the last 7/8 years. It is free.

Is anything truly free if you really want to dive into it? No, because it's taking up your time. Time is not free, so if you really want to get into the nuts and bolts of it, no, it isn't always 100% free, but you do get people out there that will give you the information you require by simply you having the ability to ask the question. So, ask away.

How shall I prepare for opportunities?

You don't. The best thing about opportunities is that you never know when they are going to appear. Some of the most successful relationships we now have, and some of the biggest businesses we now own, are from opportunities that we didn't even see coming. You can't prepare for them all of the time. So, I would say the best way to prepare in general is to be yourself and not put on a front, not put on a show. And if there are opportunities that present themselves to you, it's because of what you are doing naturally. So, I wouldn't say preparation is that important. Now, once you have the opportunity and it comes to you, then you can begin to prepare.

Which beginners' property books would you recommend?

It totally depends on what niche you are looking for. Property books are all very well, and I would recommend that you start with certain books that Rob Moore and Mark Homer have written – *The 44 Most Closely Guarded Property Secrets*. It is a very good introduction to property.

However, I think we need to start looking at property as a product, if you like, and it's everything around that, that makes the big difference. So, how you leverage your time, your mindset, your attitude, your efficiency, your organisation – stuff like that will help feed into property. So, yeah, start with that book but essentially you need to be taking action as opposed to reading too much anyway.

Which property strategy should I follow?

I don't want to use this phrase too much, but it does depend. It depends. It depends on your financial situation, depends on where you are in the country. For us, and I can only speak on our experience, we like and always have loved vanilla buy-to-lets. They are not very expensive, you can purchase them at a fairly rapid rate, they are tangible, you can see the profit, they are easy to manage so, for me, buy-to-lets are a great entry system into the world of property – but, you may not have the disposable income to put down x amount for a deposit. So, something like rent or rent-to-rent or rent-to-SA may be a more viable option.

So, it does depend on personal circumstances.

How do I get the properties I want?

By buying them. It's not rocket science. I mean, if you see a property you want to buy – all too often I hear the 'I don't have enough money' – well you are not looking, you're not looking for the money, you're not looking for the funds, you are not developing a strategy that will enable you to buy that property. It sounds harsh but if you find something you want, if you want it that badly you'll figure out a way how to obtain it.

What kind of money do I need to get my first property?

None. You don't need any money. You can find investors that have money and would like to work with you. In essence, you don't need a single penny. There is plenty of money out there It's just a case of tapping into the right resources with the right people in the right circles.

How can I find people I can trust to give me the right guidance?

I don't think you do find them; I think it naturally develops. There have been a lot of business partners that myself and my business partner have come across over the 20 odd years that we have known each other, not just in property, that have come together and split up. I think it's a wonderful thing when it does work, but I don't think you have to actively go out and find someone. If it's going to happen it will happen organically and naturally and I would just wait for it.

2. Alex Sapala

About Alex

Alex is a UK-based family man turned prolific property investor and developer, specialising in NMLI (No Money Left In) strategies including HMOs, semi-commercial and commercial conversions and BTLs. As an award-winning chartered accountant and author of The No.1 Amazon bestseller, *The Business Path to Wealth Creation*, he shares business and financial information as well as capturing people's inspirational stories through his 'Business, Wealth and Mindset' podcast. He is an accomplished investment banker with experience from some of the world's renowned financial institutions, including The Royal Bank of Scotland (RBS), Deloitte and JP Morgan. Alex is also a mentor, coach, trainer and founder of Elite Edge Wealth Academy and is passionate about mindset, knowledge sharing and financial empowerment.

Based	London
Investment location	The Midlands (predominantly)
Strategies	Specialities: Single lets, HMOs, Commercial and Semi-Commercial, Add-Value Buy-Refurb-Refinance and Commercial to Residential; Mindset and Financial Empowerment
Favourite sayings/ affirmations/mottos or key learnings you would like to share with readers	• Feel the fear and do it anyway • Whatever the mind can conceive and believe, the mind can achieve • Go out there, experience, learn and GROW

Age 43

Job (if in a job previously)

Auditor and Investment Banker.

Why did you leave your job?

To live life on my terms – to use my financial and TIME freedom to do things highest on my list of values, such as financial empowerment through knowledge sharing, as manifested in my book writing, podcast hosting and coaching and mentoring work.

What do you love about your life now?

The financial and TIME freedom to inspire and empower others through knowledge sharing and mindset shift.

Education, training, learning?

- Chartered Accountant
- Investment banker
- MINDSET
- Property Mastermind

- University of Life

Favourite books

- George S. Clason, *The Richest Man in Babylon*
- Napoleon Hill, *Success Through A Positive Mental Attitude*
- Napoleon Hill, *Think and Grow Rich*
- Ichiro Kishimi and Fumitake Koga, *The Courage To Be Disliked*

Contact details

Website: www.alexsapala.com

Alex's Answers

How do I choose the right education, training and learning for me?

In property, your choice of learning will always be on the back of choosing your strategy. This is because if, for instance, you are going for serviced accommodation, the learning more suited to you will be in networks or groups of people in masterminds who are doing serviced accommodation, and so on.

Once you have chosen a strategy, block out everything else at the beginning because it will be noise and a distraction. For example, if somebody comes to you with an HMO strategy when you're doing SA that can distract you from the path that you are pursuing and overwhelm you. You may end up dropping what you are doing and not make progress. Stick to your strategy, get better at it, achieve results and then you can look at other stuff later on along your journey.

One very important ingredient to your success is your personal development learning – those personal development books and podcasts. PD is key in bringing you into the right mindset, no matter what strategy you are doing.

What happens when I start learning and realise there's more I don't know than I do know, or that there's too much to learn?

Just take a step back but keep going – 'feel the fear and do it anyway', as they say, because there is always more to learn. Pace yourself and categorise your learning into specifics.

One of the techniques is to look at the 7 Areas of Life:

- Mental/learning/personal development
- Vocational/career/business
- Physical
- Financial
- Spiritual
- Social
- Family

On any given day and time, whatever you're learning and however you're spending your time, think of which particular area across the seven above it is aligned to, and if you're missing some of those areas in terms of your learning then there are gaps you can address.

Learning never stops, we're always learning because the environment is always changing so we need to keep pace with the changing environment. Sometimes the things you learnt years ago may have become redundant now, so just keep adapting because change is the only constant – keep going but bear in mind the 7 Areas of Life and create a balance.

How can I use my thoughts to help me do what I want?

Everything begins with a thought. If you look at your mobile phone, or your pen, or anything around you, all of that began with someone thinking of something. Thought is the origination of everything because those thoughts get turned into ideas and those ideas will eventually be put into a concept and end up being a particular thing. Thoughts are real things even though they are not physical or tangible, they have energy just like anything else and wherever your focus is, there shall your energy go.

If you think of your thoughts as energy, the more you direct them (remember the natural laws, 'energy is never lost or created it just changes from one form to another') to your goals, the more focus you're going to get and therefore the higher your chances of achieving it. Imagine this – if you have a 100 energy and you use 90 of that on good thoughts it means you only have 10 left for bad thoughts, so you are in good stead. The more you direct your energy to good, the less of it is available for bad, simple.

Whatever you are thinking about will determine your vibration; the awareness of your vibration will create your feeling and your feelings will feed into your actions and those actions will determine your results. So, work backwards – if you want certain results, the actions and the vibrations will be determined by your thoughts.

Use your thoughts wisely because in the end when you look at the flow, your thoughts will drive your results. It works both ways, if you have bad thoughts of bad things always coming to you, you put yourself in a negative vibration – you don't do anything and that gets reflected in areas that you'll end up not achieving anything. That is quite powerful because thoughts and the mind don't distinguish between what is real and what is not; whatever you instil in your subconscious will find the path of least resistance to deliver that to you. Good thoughts get positive results.

How do I know which people to connect with to help me?

People whose stories are more in alignment with you and your journey and values. That will be the distinguishing factor. If you look on social media, there are hundreds of people doing all sorts of things around the area you want to go, so in the end, go for the one whose story is more in alignment with yourself, your journey, your values. These are the people that will give you the belief and inspiration that they have your best interests at heart and will help you to move from A to B.

Is free help real help for me?

It can be. Sometimes people don't value what they don't pay for so, in the end, it's probably down to your intuition. I know when I started, I could have used people helping me even if deferred payment was demanded – I would have taken that. Sometimes free help can also be worth every penny. What I would say is, the person offering the free help is key, they need to have real experience in what you are learning from them. So, in the end strike a balance and follow your intuition.

How shall I prepare for opportunities?

Preparation for opportunities is like luck – it's discussed in *The Richest Man in Babylon*.

Preparedness is equipping yourself with the knowledge, understanding and mindset that puts you on the right vibration and frequency for you to tune into and identify the relevant opportunities when they arrive. For example, if I say I would like to do a commercial deal worth £10m this year and I just go about my journey, if I'm on a train or somewhere on a train station and there is a big poster about land and development, because my vibration is right, I am more likely to link my frequency and development with that poster and then take action to contact the people. So, just get yourself ready with the right mindset and knowledge skills and your subconscious will deliver you what you need following the path of least path of resistance.

Which beginners' property books would you recommend?

The one that comes to mind is Kevin McDonnell's *No Money Down*, and also *Right First Time Property Investing the Trilith Way* by John Foster. *Multiple Streams of Property Income* by Rob Moore gives a good grounding of what is available so you can choose the strategy that is in alignment with your values. In order to setup yourself with the right intentions and business understanding, I'd recommend my own book, the Amazon No.1 Bestseller, *The Business Path to Wealth Creation*.

Which property strategy should I follow?

Your strategy should be on the backdrop of your values as a person, and there is an exercise in *The Business Path to Wealth Creation* to help you determine that. For example, if you are someone who loves having guests around and clearing up and making things ready and lovely for people, then serviced accommodation is more likely to be for you because you are more in tune with the serviced accommodation kind of strategy.

If you are someone who absolutely hates the idea of interacting with tenants and dealing with problems like boilers not working, then the standard buy-to-let where you let agents take care of everything and you just receive your money on a monthly basis is probably more suited to you.

How do I get the properties I want?

Network with the right people and have the right systems in mind. Once you determine which ones you like, create the right support system. That includes sourcers, estate agents or more traditional or non-conventional ways, such as auctions or gumtrees or county courts (for repossessions). Get training, experience and learning in your chosen strategy area and master that, then you'll get the properties.

What kind of money do I need to get my first property?

You need money to purchase or refurbish, even if it's not a purchasing strategy. The amount will be strategy dependent, but the key thing is it doesn't have to be your own money. You can use private finance. This has got a lot of benefits compared to conventional finance such as the terms with people, you can agree all of that.

THE 1ST PLACE.

If you are buying a buy-to-let, your standard requirement will be at least 25% deposit. If it's HMO or stuff that needs work or conversions, then you need more money, but some of the strategies, such as rent-to-rent or deal sourcing, you probably won't need as much money to make a start. With deal sourcing, you just need to build up the knowledge to go find the deals and sell them. With rent-to-rent you can take on control of properties without needing to put in a load of cash; you may just need enough for redecorating.

So, depending on your strategy you may need more or less money, but the key thing is you can use other people's money. If you think of the value that you are creating, and creating win–win scenarios, someone who is getting a bad return on their money in the bank may be willing to lend you their money for a better return. You're leveraging their money and they are leveraging you by making their money work harder.

How can I find people I can trust to give me the right guidance?

Trust is a currency in almost anything, more so in business. You can find people you can trust through recommendations from people they have worked with; you can follow them on social media and see what they've done; and you can even shadow people to see exactly what they do. Just don't take people at their word – try to get the actual proof of what they have done. Visit them; go to their seminars or conferences, their investment areas. That will build the trust and connection, but recommendations are key, especially if they come from people you already trust. Reviews online and social media can count for something as well.

3. Andrew Batt

About Andrew

Andrew has over 25 years of business and property investing experience operating on both sides of the fence, as property investor and landlord, with first-hand experience as both. Andrew is an ex-property draftsman, general builder and classic and historic race car transporter, with a knack for setting up companies that are service driven in order to help others, and a passion for anything property-, business- or people-related. Andrew is also the CEO of World Game-Changers CIC, a director of multiple businesses, a public speaker and a connector.

Based	Crawley, West Sussex
Investment location	Crawley, Eastbourne, Worthing
Strategies	BRR, Commercial – Residential Conversions, Developments; Creative – No Money Down, Deal Packaging & Sourcing
Favourite sayings/ affirmations/mottos	Charge On – Today I strive to be a better person than I was yesterday, but not as good a person as I will be tomorrow.
Three key learnings you would like to share with readers	• The Power of your success lies within partnerships. • It is essential to have a mentor and or coach. • Paying for education around investing is better value than learning the hard way (which generally will cost you more).

Age 45

Job (if in a job previously)

Car park installation.

Why did you leave your job?

Because I couldn't give investing my full attention whilst having my day job.

What do you love about your life now?

I have freedom to learn, expand my network, produce results that are directly correlated to the action that I take myself – I am back in the driving seat of my entrepreneurial adventure.

Education, training, learning?

Property Education via Progressive Property, Deal Packaging to Mastermind Level, NMD Training, HMO PRO Training, Progressive Academy, plus general building knowledge from my life working on multiple projects in the UK and Europe, from refurbs to construction sites.

Favourite books

- Robert T. Kiyosaki, *Rich Dad Poor Dad*
- Kevin McDonnell, *No Money Down Property Investing*
- Brian P. Moran, *The 12 Week Year*
- Alex Sapala, *The Business Path to Wealth Creation*

THE 1ST PLACE.

- Marcus Sheridan, *They Ask You Answer*
- Ivan Misner PhD, Brian Hilliard, *Networking Like a Pro*

Contact details

Email: drew@solverpropertysolutions.co.uk

Website: www.andrewbatt.com

Linktree: https://linktr.ee/andrewbatt

Andrew's Answers

How do I choose the right education, training and learning for me?

Research and the phrase 'Due Diligence' that will come up often in your journey. Choose the right things for you by doing due diligence on the training company, looking at the results it gets and the results of others who have done the course before you. By carrying out your due diligence you can decide which is going to be your best fit.

What happens when I start learning and realise there's more I don't know than I do know, or that there's too much to learn?

You get excited because (1) you don't need to learn it all because that is what your network is for – to help you out and to help your growth. And (2) you won't ever know it all, no one knows it all, so don't waste your mind space and your brain power worrying about it. Just stick to learning what you want to learn and being guided by those around you.

How can I use my thoughts to help me do what I want?

Your thoughts create manifestations, and your manifestations create a kind of road map for you of where you want to go and what you want to do. So, you need to be mindful of your thoughts as it's very easy to say, 'I want to do everything', but then you achieve nothing because that overwhelm creeps in again. Use your thoughts wisely and slow down to speed up, just letting different thoughts manifest for a while and take you and be part of your guide for your journey or your adventure.

How do I know which people to connect with to help me?

The more you go to networking meetings, the more people you connect with, the more you will understand who you align to or who aligns to you. It will also depend on what strategy you are looking at within your journey because if you want to go into buy-to-let, there is no point aligning yourself with a bunch of people that do 10, 20, 30, 100-unit developments because they are not doing the same thing as you or they are not doing what you would like to do. But get into network events and talking to either the network hosts or co-hosts, and the admin crew because those people generally know most people that go to those events.

Is free help real help for me?

In the short term in can be, but in the long term you need to invest in yourself because no one gives you a house for free. I know that's a bit of a sweeping statement. But in general, no one is just going to walk up to you and give you a free house, so you have to work for it, you have to exchange something for it. So, free help only goes so far – you need to invest in yourself initially and your future self will thank you for doing it.

How shall I prepare for opportunities?

I'm not sure you can. I personally don't prepare for opportunities, I just grab hold of them as and when they arise.

Which beginners' property books would you recommend?

Some of the ones I have mentioned already. Alex Sapala's *The Business Path to Wealth Creation*. Also, *Routine Equals Results* and *Multiple Streams of Property Income* by Rob Moore, and *Right First Time Property Investing, The Trilith Way* by John Foster.

Which property strategy should I follow?

That depends on what your background is and what experience you bring to the table. This doesn't have to be property, it can be business experience. It depends on what you are looking to do as well. So, if you are looking to replace income quickly there is rent-to-rent, so you can do rent-to-rent serviced accommodation or rent-to-rent HMOs. If you're looking more long term then there is buy-to-let. It entirely depends on what you are trying to achieve and once you know this, you can work backwords and figure out what strategy is best suited to that because some strategies are short-term business plans.

Rent-to-rent is a great idea but most people I know rent 5–7 properties and run 5–7-year tenures, which means that the business model is going to last 5–7 years. If you can buy a buy-to-let and you can sit on it then it can go on forever.

How do I get the properties I want?

By going out there and finding them.

What kind of money do I need to get my first property?

I would say, if you've got around £3,000, or you can get together between £3,000 and up to £100,000, then you are on your way because you can either look at using the £3,000 to get your training done, and then you'll understand more, make more connections and see there is potential that you can look at moving down the 'no money down' route because you have the knowledge and the time to carry out the deal. So, I would say minimum entry you would want to have at least £3,000 and maximum it doesn't really matter it depends on what you are doing.

How can I find people I can trust to give me the right guidance?

That is down to judgement, your own judgement around people, so get to networking meetings, online or in person. Start following different people and see what they are doing and how they are doing it but obviously be mindful on social media because anyone can put anything up. You can stand by a shiny car or outside the gates of a big house and people think it's yours and you are big and successful. You need to see consistency and follow people for a period of time. But recommendations for me is the biggest – personal recommendations of someone who has actually trodden the path ahead that you want to go down.

4. Caroline Borg

About Caroline

Caroline worked at GSK for 28 years as a Medical Governance Systems Manager, where she was responsible for risk mitigation, systems and processes, managing global software development projects, training, validation and compliance, audit responses, global teams and GDPR compliance. She was the site lead for LGBTQ+ employee group.

Caroline started investing in property in 2002 and got married in 2018. She has eight dogs and eight cats – all rescues. Caroline is the co-host of SSAS Experience Network with Doug James and Invest Like a Pro training with Manish Kataria. She has a portfolio value of £1m and growing...

Based	Dousland, near Yelverton, west Devon
Investment location	Devon and Cornwall
Strategies	Commercial/Mixed Used Property
Favourite sayings/ affirmations/mottos	• Begin with the end in mind • You are competing with yourself, no one else
A key learning you would like to share with readers	• Research, do your due diligence, never assume anything, get yourself educated

Age 55

Job (if in a job previously)

Medical Governance Systems Manager for GSK.

Why did you leave your job?

So I could get access to my SSAS pension and invest in property full time and live where I wanted in the UK. I wanted to spend time doing what I wanted to do and have more time for family, friends and pets.

What do you love about your life now?

I love the challenge of learning new things and stretching myself; continual personal development; my financial freedom; being able to create a life by design; being answerable to no one else; helping others where I live.

Education, training, learning

- BSc – Business and Computing – 1st Class
- Mike Frisby – Property Business Accelerator (2019–present)
- Natasha Collins – Members Club and Asset Management (2021–present)
- Inside Property Investing Podcast

Favourite books

- Brian P. Moran, *The 12 Week Year*

- Gary Keller, *The ONE Thing*
- Angela Duckworth, *Grit*
- Darren Hardy, *The Compound Effect*

Contact details

Website: admireproperty.co.uk

Email: : caroline.a.borg@hotmail.co.uk

Caroline's Answers

How do I choose the right education, training and learning for me?

I went to some local property meetings. I was lucky there were quite a few in my location. If you resonate with the group, what will happen is that group will become your tribe and will support you. Do some research, look at things like property tribes, speak to the back office, see who you resonate with.

It's also about cost, whether you gel with someone and what they're teaching. There's no point going on a course about HMOs if that's not something you're interested in. Sometimes it can be about location. I lived in London, and going to Birmingham or Peterborough was not as appealing as exploring London.

What happens when I start learning and realise there's more I don't know than I do know, or that there's too much to learn?

It's a journey of personal development. What you need to do is focus on what you need to learn and what your goals are, so that you're learning the things you need rather than everything. This journey of personal development is like opening up a Pandora's box. There are so many books on the shelf and you think, 'How can I possibly read all of these?'

Begin with the end in mind. Think about what you want to achieve and then focus on how you're going to get there. Break it into small manageable chunks and learn mindset, but also read about the particular subject you want to learn and also listen to podcasts. When I was in my corporate job, I used my time effectively when I was travelling to work, so I'd listen to audio books and podcasts in the car.

How can I use my thoughts to help me do what I want?

The other thing you could do is affirmations in the morning. Use your thoughts and say I am going to achieve this, I am going to X, I am going to do Y. It's important with your mindset to be positive, think about what you're grateful for as well. Create a gratitude list and write three things you're grateful for every day.

How do I know which people to connect with to help me?

Once you start to mix in property circles, you will connect with relevant people. Go to local meetings. You're really lucky compared to people 20–30 years ago because you have the internet to help you. Google property meetings near your postcode. Find out what that is, go and mix with people and find feedback.

THE 1ST PLACE.

Property Tribes is a really good resource of things you could find out. Read books, listen to things. I used to go to the property investor show in London at the Excel centre and that was a good source of information – seeing people presenting, see who you like, see who you resonate with.

Is free help real help for me?

It's a bit of a loaded question because, while sometimes things are free, it's an upline to something else. You might go to a webinar that's free, but it will be an upline to sell a course. I find that in the property community there are a lot of people who have achieved and they're a very giving community. They like to help people, so you can reach out to people, and then talk to and share their experience and advice.

Free help in some resources can be very helpful though. Why do something yourself that you've never done, if you can learn from somebody who's trodden that path before?

How shall I prepare for opportunities?

Think about what you're trying to achieve and just be ready. Somebody might say, 'there's this property that might be useful for you to see' so make sure you jump on it right away before anybody else gets to see that property.

Be ready with all your financial information, so when you have to get a mortgage it's easy to go forward with. It's important to have the systems and processes in place, so you're not panicking, and everything gets done last minute. By doing things and pacing yourself, everything will be ready when you need it to be.

Which beginners' property books would you recommend?

I was quite inspired by *Property Magic* by Simon Zutshi. I know there are various editions of it, but it tells you simple ways in which you can do things. I've shared that book with three different people who are interested in property as a way to get started.

Which property strategy should I follow?

That really depends on the person. If you're working in a corporate job, the chances are you might be happy in your job so you can say, 'In 10 years' time I'll leave my job.' You might say, 'Buy-to-let is a good strategy. I'll buy 10 buy-to-lets, so in 10 years' time I will have reached my target and replaced my income.'

If you're wanting to accelerate that and you want to make your income quite quickly you might consider other strategies like HMOs, serviced accommodation (where people use Airbnb to come and stay in your property). Those will get you more income, but they also require more intense work. If you're in a corporate job, you have to decide whether you want to do that or whether someone else can help you. The other thing that people don't necessarily consider is commercial properties because your commercial tenants often have fully repaired and insuring leases, which means less hassle for you.

How do I get the properties I want?

You need to make sure you have laser sharp focus on what you need to get. Then you have to be very persistent. Be consistent, do something every day to get you to your goal and just keep plodding along. If a particular strategy is new to you, work with people who can help you get there

– be it training, asset management, mentorship. Work with people who you know have done that before.

Some people are quite creative, they can just go and try things and make mistakes, but it depends on your personality. Try the Wealth Dynamics profiling. You can take a Wealth Dynamics assessment and that helps you understand what your strengths and weaknesses are. It's quite telling and will help you determine who you need to help you.

What kind of money do I need to get my first property?

Some people can get the money from a re-mortgage or borrow the money from the bank of mum and dad, or from friends, but it also depends on what type of property you're buying. If you're buying a buy-to-let property in the Northeast and it costs, say £75,000, you might only need £40,000 to buy it. But if you're buying a property in Mayfair for £3 million, you're going to need more money. It really depends on what you're doing.

Personally, I don't like working with investors for money until I've had experience in what I'm doing. Other people will say, 'yeah, I'm happy to get investor's money even though I've got no experience in this strategy.' We're all different.

How can I find people I can trust to give me the right guidance?

This can be quite difficult. Make sure you mix with people, set up groups in WhatsApp, join Facebook groups and find out about the good and bad guys/girls in this business. There will always be people who've got more experience than you and there will be always people who have less experience than you. Help people who have less experience than you but learn from people who have more experience. Keep up with training, mentoring, reading, and podcasts – it's all there on the internet.

5. Craig Phillips

About Craig

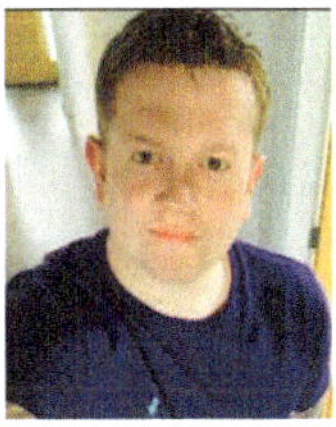

I'm an accidental landlord, who did everything wrong and made many, many mistakes along the way. I got into property education and realised that I had a thirst for property investment, so I threw myself in at the deep end. I started with a few buy-to-lets and flips before becoming too big for my boots and jumping into new build developments without knowing what I was getting into. Many expensive lessons later, I survived (just) and now take those lessons with me into every new project I'm involved with. Now a mentor on Progressive Property's flagship training package, I love giving knowledge and experiences to people so they don't make the same mistakes that I did.

Based	North Yorkshire
Investment location	North Yorkshire / Lincoln
Strategies	New Build, Commercial Conversions, BTL
Favourite sayings/ affirmations/mottos	You never fail until you stop trying – Albert Einstein
Three key learnings you would like to share	• Take your time, this is not a race • Make sure your numbers are right • Measure twice, cut once

Job (if in a job previously)

Military.

Why did you leave your job?

I wanted to be in charge of my future, and not live month to month.

What do you love about your life now?

I have the freedom to do what I want, when I want.

Education, training, learning

- Progressive Property Masterclass, and many other courses
- Learning from my own mistakes (boots on the ground learning)
- Now a mentor for Progressive Property

Favourite books

- Susan Jeffers, *Feel the Fear and Do It Anyway*
- Robert T. Kiyosaki, *Rich Dad Poor Dad*
- Rob Moore, *Multiple Streams of Property Income*
- Seth Godin, *The Dip*

Contact details

Email: craig@cceoproperty.com

Craig's Answers

How do I choose the right education, training and learning for me?

You have to go and sample a few companies or people or books or whatever. See who you feel more comfortable with. At the end of the day, you are going to be trusting these people with a lot of money so you have to feel comfort and a synergy with that company or person.

What happens when I start learning and realise there's more I don't know than I do know, or that there's too much to learn?

If you are a beginner and you realise there's too much to learn, you've learnt your first lesson straight away because you will never ever know everything. So, I would say take it in small bite-size chunks and keep revaluating where you are at certain times and who you have helping to teach and train you.

How can I use my thoughts to help me do what I want?

Your thoughts are everything! It's your mindset that will get you through challenges and it's your mindset that will make you shrivel up and die. So, always remember

- it's your thoughts and the way you look at what you are potentially doing that is going to get you through any situation.
- it's your mind that is a driving factor and nothing else

How do I know which people to connect with to help me?

I would say go with people that have proof of concept, so you can

- see what they've done
- hear how they did it
- actually go and touch the building, the property, whatever it may be

So basically, you can see the results of their hard work. Don't necessarily go with people who have not done that yet.

Is free help real help for me?

Free help is just as good or bad as paid help. You can't actually say what's good and what's bad until you try doing it. There are people that have given me lessons for free that I've learnt a lot more from than when I've paid thousands for a course. As long as you take it inside and learn from it, it doesn't matter if it's free or paid. Both have their benefits, and both have their curses.

How shall I prepare for opportunities?

I would say if you're intending to get investing then start by speaking to the team that are going to help you get these things over the line. Your solicitors, your agents, your brokers, your accountant – the basic team around you. Speak to those people first.

THE 1ST PLACE.

Which beginners' property books would you recommend?

It's all about mindset and, again, I'd say Rob Moore's *Multiple Streams of Property Income* is a good beginner book. However, all the basic property books for beginners are good at the first stage.

Which property strategy should I follow?

The one that you can see yourself doing in 5–10 years' time, not one you can only see yourself doing for 1 or 2 years. What you want to do is focus on the strategy that gives you your long-term goal and then get really good at that, and that financially frees you up to potentially do other things in the future. Envision where you are in 10 years' time first and then do that one.

How do I get the properties I want?

By speaking to agents and telling them exactly what you want and what you are in the market for, depending on whatever strategy you are involved in. Start speaking to agents first and see what their feedback is.

What kind of money do I need to get my first property?

So, money can be

- from your own personal bank account
- from releasing funds
- from refinancing your own house
- from investor finance, maybe friends and family

It doesn't matter where it comes from as long as you do the due diligence properly and make sure the deal is actually a deal and you know the numbers inside and out.

How can I find people I can trust to give me the right guidance?

I would say use word of mouth. Speak to people who have used them in the past, see what results they got and if they actually lived up to what they were promising they could provide.

6. Darren Burrows

About Darren

For 30 years Darren has set up and run start-ups and SME businesses. Over the past 17 years he's run subcontract firms at director level in the construction and FM sectors.

Darren has delivered refurb and renovation projects since 2007 and, as well as being an investor, has worked with other property business owners to help them plan, structure and manage refurb projects to stay totally legal and compliant – something that most property training courses don't cover. Darren also has his own YouTube channel: Darren Burrows – Taurus Property Group.

Based	Bromley, Kent
Investment location	UK
Strategies	Refurb, conversions, BRR, Tenant Buyers, R2SA, looking for new build plots/sites to develop
Favourite sayings/ affirmations/mottos	• Make sure your ladder is up against the right wall • Assumption is the mother of all f#ck-ups
Three key learnings you would like to share with readers	• Never take anyone at face value • Follow your gut feeling – it's normally right • Never rush into things without due diligence

Age 50

Job (if in a job previously)

Commercial & Operations Director at SME companies – in and around the construction and facilities management sectors since 2005.

Why did you leave your job?

Redundancy.

What do you love about your life now?

Freedom to make choices and work on my own terms.

Education, training, learning

- Progressive Property – Masterclass, No Money Down, Deal Packaging, B2S
- Unlimited Success – ESD, Social Media Masterclass
- SuperGenius – Wealth Workshop

Favourite books

- Robert T. Kiyosaki, *Rich Dad, Poor Dad*
- David Goggins, *Can't Hurt Me*
- Darren Hardy, *The Compound Effect*

THE 1ST PLACE.

Contact details

Website: www.taurus-property.com

Linktree: https://linktr.ee/darrenburrows

Email: info@darrenburrows.co.uk

Darren's Answers

How do I choose the right education, training and learning for me?

Do plenty of research – look at social media, look at YouTube, look at all the big training companies. Even the smaller trading companies have a presence on most platforms. Do your research, read reviews, join their Facebook groups if they have them and get a bit of a feel of what they're like. Get to know their attitudes, what makes them tick and their kind of way of presenting as well. At the end of the day a lot of the content is fairly similar, but you've got to be able to resonate with the individual trainers. The last thing you want to be doing is sitting in a room for two or three days with trainers that you just don't gel with. So, do your research and know who you're going to be working with.

What happens when I start learning and realise there's more I don't know than I do know, or that there's too much to learn?

I think that's always going to be a challenge with doing a course, because there's always more to learn and every day is like a school day. People who've been in property for years are still learning every day. You're never going to stop learning, it's just a case of trying not to get overwhelmed by it. Break it down again, look at what you're learning, put it into action as quickly as you can, and then you'll understand and get to know: which parts of it you enjoy doing; which parts you don't enjoy; which parts you're good at and then you can take it forward with that in mind.

How can I use my thoughts to help me do what I want?

I'm a big one for gut feeling. I'm quite a good judge of character, so I'll always go with whatever I'm feeling at the time. I'll keep in mind how something is going to help me progress and serve me, and stay focused. Just know what you want from it and just always be thinking about that and have that in the back of your mind all the time.

How do I know which people to connect with to help me?

In the early stages I'd advise that you try to connect with as many people as possible. As you go through your journey and you get to know people better, there will be some people that you get on with and some people you don't. There's nothing wrong with that – that's just life. In the initial stages (certainly in my experience when I first started in property full time) connect with everybody. I spent probably two years doing that.

I had a lot of conversations, met a lot of people, went out to networking meetings and again there will be some people that you just naturally get drawn to. You need to have a lot of people going into your funnel at the top from your connections point of view and then ultimately you will find people that you want to be working with longer term.

Is free help real help for me?

There's a lot of free content out there, and a saying that, 'free advice is worth every penny'. Try to absorb, understand and take on board as much of it as you can before you start. Obviously, research coaching, mentoring, training etc too, but there's a lot of free content out there and it's definitely worth taking advantage of that.

How shall I prepare for opportunities?

Always be open-minded. Again, this kind of depends where you're at on your journey. In the early stages, or during a period where you haven't got a lot going on, be open to opportunity and try to filter that to find out how well something is going to suit you and what you're looking to achieve. From a preparation point of view, always be open minded and willing to talk to people and have those conversations.

Which beginners' property books would you recommend?

There's a good book by Rob Moore and Mark Homer called *Property Investing Secrets*. Also, a book by one of my mentors, Kevin McDonnell, called *No Money Down Property Investing*. It's a great book if you're looking to do stuff that's a little more creative – it's full of creative strategies.

Which property strategy should I follow?

You should do the strategy that fits with your end goals, and, to a degree, what works in your particular area. A lot of people think that property investing only works in certain areas, when in fact it works in every area – it's just that some different strategies may work in different areas better. So, I always recommend that you understand what you're trying to achieve first, or at least get a fairly good idea, and then work backwards from that to focus on certain strategies.

How do I get the properties I want?

It's just a case of putting in the leg work – speak to agents, do the viewings, put in the offers. It's always key to make sure you offer on everything that you look at. Most of your offers won't be accepted, but some will so just be *very* clear on your numbers. Again, work backwards from what your exit strategy is.

So, if you're looking for a buy-to-let property – understand what that looks like, and what costs will be associated with that refurb and all your legal costs. Work it all backwards making sure those numbers are in the structure of the deal and if it all stacks up then just keep hammering at it. All of this stuff is just a numbers game, so you've got to keep on going, keep on going and eventually something will drop.

What kind of money do I need to get my first property?

The amount of money will vary depending on the property itself and where it is. Typically, you're probably going to need a 25% deposit, plus your refurb cost, plus your legal fees and associated costs. There are times when you might be able use bridging finance or look to find investors to work with (then the investors will bring the money to the opportunity and you just have to put the numbers together to make sure there's a deal). It varies from property to property.

THE 1ST PLACE.

How can I find people I can trust to give me the right guidance?

So my advice on this would be to look at social proof. Look at what they're doing on social media, get to know them on video, get to know them on YouTube and get testimonials from people. Try to speak to other people that have either been on their training or have worked with them as coaches or mentors. It's the same as if you were looking at a property opportunity – you need to do your due diligence and make sure you're comfortable and that they fit with what you're looking to do.

7. Darren Grigas

About Darren

After struggling to run a single mile following a car accident, Darren defiantly progressed to running ultra-marathons across deserts, jungles, and 100-mile frozen lakes, proving to himself and others just how resilient humans can be with the right mindset and knowledge. Those experiences and lessons have positively impacted all areas of his life, and shaped it into one he never anticipated, but is truly grateful for. Darren has negotiated five Rent-to-Serviced-Accommodation opportunities, turning over around £200k per annum. He also has his own YouTube channel.

Two recent projects:

Wine Bar:

- Purchase price £135k: converted into four units, let as 3x BTL and 1x SA
- Development costs £75k, new value £330k: Rents: £25,500pa
- The single SA unit takes around £20k pa

Off-market deal – two-bed listed cottage:

- Purchase price £45k,
- Refurb spend; £33k, value today: £200k
- Mortgage at £119k, rent = £9k pa

Based	Peterborough
Investment location	Peterborough & Stamford areas
Strategies	BRR/BTL, Flips, Conversions, Renovations, R2SA
Favourite sayings/ affirmations/mottos	• You don't have to go fast, or far, just go
A key learning you would like to share with readers	• Knowledge is for keeps, so invest in yourself, you are your greatest asset

Age 45

Job (if in a job previously)

Graphic Designer.

What do you love about your life now?

Flexibility, freedom, not dreading Mondays. Being able to make a positive difference to others by passing on my experiences, and providing opportunities for others to push their limits on my retreats and at the Forest Facility Adventure Centre (launching in Spring 2023).

THE 1ST PLACE.

Education, training, learning

- Deal packaging and SA courses via Progressive Property. Development has been self-taught since 2005.

Favourite books

- John J Ratey, *Spark*
- Arnold Schwarzenegger, *Total Recall*
- Hannah Critchlow, *The Science of Fate*

Contact details

Website: Darrengrigas.com

Email: darrengrigas@hotmail.com

Darren's Answers

How do I choose the right education, training and learning for me?

Get recommendations from other people, join forums and Facebook communities. Always go by customers reviews and other people's experience. If you join a Facebook property community, put a post out there and ask what people would recommend as a starting point. Ask for book recommendations, mentors and you'll get a consensus. Then, you'll get a good idea of where to start.

What happens when I start learning and realise there's more I don't know than I do know, or that there's too much to learn?

Break it down into bite-size chunks. There's always going to be more to learn, but that applies to everything in life. Try to narrow down what you can do in your first six months or first year. Don't get overwhelmed by a million different property strategies. Take on one to start with, and focus on the fundamentals. Ignore all the other stuff that's distracting and overwhelming focus on that.

How can I use my thoughts to help me do what I want?

Your thoughts apply to every part of your life from the moment you wake up, to the moment you go to sleep (some even when you're asleep). Try energy clearing. Declutter stuff that is holding you back or setting you back. Get recommendations for books and education on how to fine tune your mindset, and to think in the right way to achieve what you want to achieve.

A good book recommendation is the *Values Factor* by Dr John Demartini. That will help you determine where your core values lie. Start to alter your mindset and understand why you work the way you do, because we're all completely individual and unique. Get books on the science behind what your brain is doing, when it's doing what it's doing.

How do I know which people to connect with to help me?

It's always helpful to look to people who are a few steps ahead of where you are and in the direction of where you want to go. Follow people online for a little while, just to see how genuine they are, and connect with someone who's genuine. Make sure there's something in it for them too, rather than you just being another friend request. You've got to have a genuine, authentic reason to connect with someone, then just arrange to meet over a coffee or have a chat online, and see if you can benefit each other in some way.

Is free help real help for me?

Free help is real help, but yes, it's limited. I get a lot of people who ask me for help and advice, and I genuinely love it, because I want people to succeed. It does depend on who's delivering the help and what their goal is – if they're genuine and sincere. Ultimately if you're paying someone for help and advice then you should have a more committed amount of content.

How shall I prepare for opportunities?

If you stay ready to take an opportunity, you need the knowledge, the resources and the connections to grab it. Get educated and have a team or a network that you can call on at the drop of a hat if you need to. 'If you stay ready, you don't have to get ready.' So, be educated, primed, have your team ready to go and have a few quid in the bank if you need to or get funding arranged.

Which beginners' property books would you recommend?

Property Investing Secrets by Rob Moore and Mark Homer. That has a lot of content, a lot of different ideas. *Essential Tips to Avoid Property Taxes* by Iain Wallace was also very handy.

Which property strategy should I follow?

It depends entirely on your goals – whether you want to have a full-time job with property or if you want to make a few extra pounds or invest some savings you've got. It depends on each individual's circumstances and short, mid and long-term goals. If you want to have a safe bet, make a few pounds a month and ideally have it go up in value over the years, then a buy-to-let property is ideal.

Ideally everyone loves a below market value purchase if they can get one, but you've got to be realistic and hope that you find somewhere that needs a bit of work and you can invest in that. There are many rent-to-rent and rent-to-SA strategies that can work. It depends on what you've got to invest, what position you're in, what you want to achieve this year, next year or in the next 10 years and into retirement.

How do I get the properties I want?

To get the properties you want, you need to be looking at lots and lots of properties. You've then got to be in a position to run the numbers on it, analyse it to make sure it's a good deal that benefits you, and then know where your cut-off point is.

You don't want to get caught in a bidding war, so you need to know your numbers and how to analyse a deal. If you've built a relationship with agents and they believe in you, know that you're a genuine investor who could bring repeat business, it may help to swing things your way.

What kind of money do I need to get my first property?

It depends on what you know and who you know. If you know how to run, identify and analyse a good deal and you know at least one good investor with money who's willing to partner up with you, you potentially need no money.

THE 1ST PLACE.

How can I find people I can trust to give me the right guidance?

It all comes down to networking, meeting people, education and insight. Deciding what you need is a good way to know who you then need to connect with. You can then go on to online property communities and see what people are posting, sharing and commenting on. Get familiar with the sincerity and the genuine successes these people are having. Then reach out and connect with them or go to an open seminar or an event where you can meet with them. Always look for mutual benefits too.

8. Dave Goodfellow

About Dave

Dave is owner of Ikonic SA Ltd, mentor at Ikonic Training Academy and fellow property investor. In the past, his focus was flipping properties and he had a small buy-to-let portfolio. Starting his serviced accommodation journey was not as easy as it sounds, but having the right system and people built around his business helped him build and scale his business with over 70 properties. He is in the process of building a pipeline of ApartHotels with a total GDV of £10m.

Based	Chester
Investment location	UK
Strategies	Serviced Accommodation & ApartHotels
Favourite sayings/ affirmations/mottos	• Making data-led decisions is key to a property investor's success
Three key learnings you would like to share with readers	• Know, like and trust is so important in building long-term relationships. • Property is not a get rich quick strategy – it's a long-term process. • Consistency is key – it's the boring mundane everyday tasks that move your business forward.

Age 41

Job (if in a job previously)

Operations Director of a Home Improvements Company.

Why did you leave your job?

To spend more time with the family and be in more control of my own life.

What do you love about your life now?

Freedom and choice to do what I want when I want.

Education, training, learning

- Constantly learning daily from my relationships built over the last decade.

Favourite books

- Dale Carnegie, *How to Win Friends and Influence People*
- Napoleon Hill, *Think and Grow Rich*
- Gino Wickman, *Rocket Fuel*

Contact details

All via Linktree: https://linktr.ee/davegoodfellow

THE 1ST PLACE.

Dave's Answers

How do I choose the right education, training and learning for me?

Make sure you understand your values, what your end goal is and where you want to be in a certain period of time. The end goal is a massive thing – you build your strategy to get to your end goal. So, that's the biggest thing, making sure you pick a strategy within property that's going to help you get there – whether that be cash flow, capital appreciation, whatever that is, it's all about that end goal.

What happens when I start learning and realise there's more I don't know than I do know, or that there's too much to learn?

That's very much down to the person's specifics. What you tend to find in a lot of the big training companies is that they'll get you on what's called a value ladder and will make the next part quite out of reach, if that makes sense. They'll do enough training to keep you on board before you get onto the next part. What you want is a training company that gives you detailed answers for everything that you need and you shouldn't be in a position where the learning is too much. Property isn't rocket science! We're not building nuclear submarines or building rocket ships to go to the moon. It's bricks and mortar, and it's a way of controlling property to bring money into your bank account. A lot of things don't need to be over-complicated.

How can I use my thoughts to help me do what I want?

That's a very simple question with a very simple answer. You've got two voices – the voice that you use now, that you can hear, and you've got the internal voice that's talking to you on a constant basis. Listen to that internal voice to help you move yourself forward.

How do I know which people to connect with to help me?

Recommendations.

Is free help real help for me?

It depends on the person and what they want to get out of it.

How shall I prepare for opportunities?

You won't know what opportunities are available until they land on your desk, but you need to understand if an opportunity lands on your desk you need to go back to some of the questions we asked previously. You need to understand what your motive is, know your numbers and do your due diligence.

Which beginners' property books would you recommend?

Property Secrets by Rob Moore and Mark Homer, and *Property Magic* by Simon Zutshi. What those books give you is an overview of several different strategies, they don't go deep, but they'll give you a good idea.

Which property strategy should I follow?

Again, it depends on your end goal and on what position you're in. If you want to build cash flow, then using other people's property is a good one. If you want to build capital, go and learn or BRR model.

How do I get the properties I want?

Get the right education in the right area, and you'll need to go through a process of being able to make yourself credible and sell yourself. If you're using other people's properties from a cash flow perspective, you need to be able to sell yourself to them. Property is all about people and building relationships, so whether you're getting other people's property and using them to cash flow, or you're purchasing properties in the right place at the right time, it's all about building relationships with other people – it's as simple as that.

What kind of money do I need to get my first property?

You don't need any money to get into property. If you've got time, knowledge, passion and enthusiasm you can joint venture with other people. Joint venture with other people means you don't need money to get into property.

How can I find people I can trust to give me the right guidance?

You've got to build 'know', 'like' and 'trust'. Spending time, getting recommendations, seeing how those people deal with other people. It's the best way of doing it and building those relationships – 'know', 'like' and 'trust' is a massive thing.

9. David Bennett

About David

David started his career working in accountancy and wealth management for 4 years and found interest in property whilst studying civil engineering at university. Having made the move to property, David started by letting rooms out on behalf of estate agents. He also acquired and operated serviced accommodation units, and managed properties on behalf of landlords. David currently specialises in HMOs and properties with short leases.

Based	Leeds
Investment location	National
Strategies	BTL, HMO
Favourite saying	Progress not perfection
Three key learnings you would like to share with readers	• Be crystal clear on what you want to achieve in the long-term aka a life plan. Be prepared that may change and that's okay. • Don't compare yourself to other people. • Say no to things that don't fit into your life plan and be okay with saying no.

Age 28

Job (if in a job previously)

Auditor at Grant Thornton, Wealth Management.

Why did you leave your job?

For more freedom.

What do you love about your life now?

The freedom I have now.

Education, Training, Learning

- Progressive Property training.

Favourite books

- James Kerr, *Legacy*
- Jocko Willink, *Extreme Ownership*

Contact details

Email: David@bennettandco.uk

David's Answers

How do I choose the right education, training and learning for me?

I think it's really important that the course you invest in is led by someone who is currently, and successfully, investing in property. I made the mistake of going with a bigger training company but in hindsight, I would have gone to a smaller company/individual where you can get one-to-one mentoring, which I find the most beneficial.

What happens when I start learning and realise there's more I don't know than I do know, or that there's too much to learn?

I think that question applies to life in general! The more I learn, the more I realise how much more there is left to learn. I will probably never know it all, but that's okay. I would encourage everybody to continue to learn and take on new challenges because that's where professional and personal growth lies.

How can I use my thoughts to help me do what I want?

By organising your thoughts and being very clear on what you want. If you're clear on what you want, your thoughts will automatically and subconsciously start getting you there.

It's like a car with a sat nav. If your mind says, 'this is the destination', you will start coming up with a plan of how to get there.

How do I know which people to connect with to help me?

Just meet as many people as you can and see what gut feeling you're getting. Trust your instincts, and if you have any reservations or doubt, go with your gut.

Is free help real help for me?

Yes. Some of the most valuable things I've learnt have been free. Don't be naïve though. It's common for people to give you something for free to demonstrate knowledge and then ask you to pay for the 'golden nugget'.

How shall I prepare for opportunities?

Be clear on what you want to gain from the opportunity. Then do everything you can to prepare yourself and acquire knowledge relating to that field.

Which beginners' property books would you recommend?

The Progressive Property book *No Money Down* by Kevin McDonnell. I thought it was good for telling you a lot about different strategies. Don't be fooled into thinking that 'no money down' exists, however. There always needs to be money down whether it's yours or someone else's.

Which property strategy should I follow?

Be very clear on what your current skills and limitations are. Be aware of your available resources and your appetite for risk. Once you have established those, the property strategy will be a bit clearer.

THE 1ST PLACE.

How do I get the properties I want?

Be clear on the types of property you want and reverse engineer it. Think about what the property can give you, for example, replacing income and building wealth.

What kind of money do I need to get my first property?

Be clear on what property you want. Different properties cost different amounts. For example, an HMO will need a lot more than a standard two-bed terrace in the north.

How can I find people I can trust to give me the right guidance?

I think that is a very difficult question to answer. It takes time and trial and error to find the right connections. Don't underestimate the power of networking and recommendations.

10. Debbie Sheriff

About Debbie

Debbie Sherriff repurposes old defunct buildings and turns them into beautiful opulent short stays or co-living spaces. A grandmother now, Debbie started her career as midwife, both the UK and Middle East and left this space during lockdown to pursue her dream. During Debbie's nursing career, she raised three children and completed a degree at Bournemouth University. Today Debbie is continuing with property education and builds her love of interior design and spatial wellbeing.

Based	Bournemouth
Investment location	Bournemouth
Strategies	Repurposing defunct buildings into opulent experiential short stays and co-living spaces
Favourite sayings/affirmations/mottos	• What doesn't kill you makes you stronger • If you say you can't, or say you can, you are probably right
Two key learnings you would like to share with readers	• Believe in yourself • Have a good power team

Age 60

Job (if in a job previously)

Midwife.

Why did you leave your job?

To work in property full time.

What do you love about your life now?

That I am free to carve out the future for myself and my family and that we, as a family, can leave a life-long legacy for generations to come.

Education, training, learning

- BSc (hons); Progressive Property Courses: BRRR, Deal packaging PP, Deal Packaging Mastermind; Self-learning around Mindset and property books, podcasts, YouTube, webinars, etc.

Favourite Books

- Mel Robbins, *The 5 Second Rule*
- Napoleon Hill, *Think and Grow Rich*
- James Clear, *Atomic Habits*

Contact details

Email: debbie.sherriff@hotmail.co.uk

Debbie's Answers

How do I choose the right education, training and learning for me?

It depends on your learning style; some people need to see and do. I'm a see and doer.

I think the whole process of property is always a learning experience and you know if you resonate with certain courses or books or mentors. It's all a very personal thing, but obviously a lot of it is you – do your due diligence if you are paying a lot of money for mentorship, for example.

What happens when I start learning and realise there's more I don't know than I do know, or that there's too much to learn?

I think you have to be willing to learn and if you're not willing to learn then perhaps it's not the right thing for you. I don't think you ever stop learning and if I thought I knew everything I don't think I would actually do it because it's not true – no one knows everything.

How can I use my thoughts to help me do what I want?

Ok, my thoughts... This is a good one for me because I'm quite good with thinking outside the box. For example, when I wanted to do serviced accommodation apartments I really liked a building, but it was a commercial building, an office. I couldn't afford flats in Bournemouth, so I bought the offices and converted them into serviced accommodation. It was a bit scary (and perhaps not best for your second project!) but I felt I had the knowledge to do this, but actually I was thinking outside the box. Just don't be blinkered, think all around you.

How do I know which people to connect with to help me?

Your network – you find groups like PPN and things like that. I listened on Clubhouse to see people I resonated with. You learn as you go along but remember, not everyone tells you the truth. Also, you learn who to like and trust and those are the people I tend to lean towards.

Is free help real help for me?

Absolutely. Though I have invested in education, I have also had a lot of free help and if I'm honest sometimes that has been more valuable. I've also given free help to people – and I think property is a very good area for this – people are usually willing to help and especially help a newbie. I definitely think it's good.

How shall I prepare for opportunities?

Research, research, research and, obviously, mindset.

Which beginners' property books would you recommend?

I think all the Progressive ones are quite clear.

Which property strategy should I follow?

One that you are going to enjoy, one that you can afford. I started out thinking I wanted to do deal packaging and realised quite quickly I don't like giving my deals away so that obviously wasn't the right strategy for me. It has to be something you love and that you are passionate about.

How do I get the properties I want?

Networking and being continuous with what you do. Keeping a pipeline, committing and being consistent and persistent.

What kind of money do I need to get my first property?

Depends on the strategy obviously, but I don't believe you can do no money down. Maybe someone can prove me wrong. I don't know but obviously the money you have available to you lends itself to what strategy you can do first. But remember you don't always have to work up towards a buy-to-let property, because if you have the money already or you've got investors then just do what you like.

How can I find people I can trust to give me the right guidance?

That's quite tricky because it's just trial and error and meeting people that you get to know, like and trust. Usually, if you pay for education, it's usually good, and it's important to do your research around people.

Sometimes people can give you guidance on property, but it's not always property related. Most of my learning that I do for myself isn't property at the moment its more about mindset because that's where my issues are. I don't really read property books that often.

11. Elizabeth Baitson

About Elizabeth

I am a serial entrepreneur connecting business owners, property professionals and UHNWI to connect, learn and grow from each other. I have multiple successful businesses, run several successful networks with thousands of members, and have coached hundreds of people to start or grow their ventures. I am passionate about wealth in all forms, not just financial but spiritual and emotional wealth, too.

Based	Warwickshire
Investment location	Worldwide
Strategies	HMO/Supported Living/BTL/R2R/SA/Development
Favourite sayings/ affirmations/mottos	• Don't bring me your problem and make it mine. • • I have a wonderful work in a wonderful way, I give wonderful service for wonderful pay.' – Florence Scovel Shinn
Three key learnings you would like to share with readers	• Relationships before business • Networking is NOT optional • • People are always the problem, and the solution

Age 43

Job (if in a job previously)

Mathematical modeller in banking, management consultancy and scientific research.

Why did you leave your job?

It was killing my soul.

What do you love about your life now?

FREEDOM and SOVEREIGNTY.

Education, training, learning?

- I studied shamanism and alternative medicine in my early 20s, which I still use today in business decisions.

Favourite books

- Eckhart Tolle, *The Power of Now*
- Florence Scovel Shinn, *The Game of Life and How to Play It*
- The Bible

Contact details

Websites: www.highnetconnect.co.uk; www.lizbaitson.com

Email: liz@highnetconnect.co.uk

Elizabeth's Answers

How do I choose the right education, training and learning for me?

The first thing you've got to do is understand exactly your life situation right now. Are you at a place where you've got a load of time on your hands? Are you at a place where you've got a load of money in your hands? You've got to figure out where you are first, and then if you don't know how to discern between types of training, I would go to somebody for free, somebody that is in that world.

Look at your network, find some people whose brains you can pick quickly, and ask the question where do I start? If anyone is doing the hard sell on you, I would say that is something to avoid. Are they interested in you and where you are, or are they interested in selling you something that's going to make them some money? That's the way I judge people, by their interest level in me.

What happens when I start learning and realise there's more I don't know than I do know, or that there's too much to learn?

I would balance every single time you are taking information in. In any kind of training environment, you have got to ask the question, 'Is this something that I'm going to be personally responsible for in my property career?' For example, if I'm learning about property development and I go on a course and find myself saying, 'Oh my goodness, I don't understand deal analysis, I don't understand surveying, I do not understand all of this', I would then ask myself, 'Are you actually learning stuff that's irrelevant to the role you're going to be taking in the future?' If the answer is yes, I would then balance my training with my networking.

You should be investing as much, if not more, in your networking as you are with your training, because you will then be building a team. Don't panic if you can't understand it or take it all in – perhaps it's not for you, and it's actually for you to find a partner that can.

How can I use my thoughts to help me do what I want?

You've got to master your thoughts for starters and realise that you are not your thoughts, you are somebody behind the thoughts. And there has to be some level of discipline. Watch the way you think and have a look at how your sympathetic and parasympathetic nervous systems drive your thoughts. What I mean by that is the kind of automatic responses that you have, that could be physiological. Dive deep into some self-reflection, because if your thoughts are mostly automatic and you find that you're not actually consciously feeling in control of them, you are never going to be able to use them to manifest.

How do I know which people to connect with to help me?

It takes time. Relationships are not to be entered into lightly. I would say, you need to follow people for probably a minimum of 6 months, and not only online but in person if you can. There's nothing like an in-person meeting to help you understand the energy of this person and then have some online interactions with them and watch the way they treat other people. If these are the kinds of people that are generous of spirit, and work like you do, then you're more likely to have a successful business relationship with them. If you are just picking people because you think they are fabulous and you want to kind of jump on their coat-tails (which I have done in the past), it's going to end in disaster, so you've really got to find like-minded people.

THE 1ST PLACE.

Is free help real help for me?

It can be. It's a difficult one, but it can be. I like to have fair exchange in all of my relationships, so free help is usually something that doesn't seem like there's a fair exchange, but for me I'm constantly looking for people to join my world and join my team.

So, when I'm giving something away for free, it's actually selfish because if they're a great person, I'm trying to get to know them and I know that. Always, always give a favour over taking the money. I give favours all the time and I don't take money and it usually works out well. You've just got to be discerning. Don't get sucked into an energy vampire relationship. You can find that free help is actually incredibly symbiotic.

How shall I prepare for opportunities?

The best way I prepare for opportunities is by being really careful when using the words YES and NO. I used to be someone that said yes to absolutely everything and then I found myself completely overwhelmed with opportunities. Now I find myself saying no to most things and actually opportunities are still coming thick and fast.

I think it's a myth to say that if you have boundaries you're cutting yourself off from opportunities. I would say the best way to be ready for opportunities is to know your boundaries and do not say yes to everything. This way, you'll find you funnel the correct opportunities to you much more effectively, and you'll then be ready to open yourself up to them as opposed to just giving your spirit away for free.

Which beginners' property books would you recommend?

For property sourcing, a book I really like for a beginner is Tina Walsh's book, *The Property Compliance Sourcing Manual*. For property development, I quite like White Box – they had a book a few years back by Andy Giraldi and Lloyd Groom that made it really nice and simple to understand the beginnings of property development.

Which property strategy should I follow?

The one that is going to cause you the least pain I would say. Think about where you are in your life. Property sourcing, for example, is called an entry level property strategy, but it takes a huge amount of time. So, if you've got the energy and time on your hands – perhaps you're a student and you've got some time off, or maybe you're retired – then yeah that's a great thing to do. But for most people, the amount of time that it takes is massive and the amount of rejections you get are massive.

Rent-to-rent is for people that have less time and less money, but it's a great entry level. Buy, refurb, refinance is a great place to be if you've got some cash to put in yourself. Otherwise, you're going to be dealing with private finance and, as a beginner, that's not always easy.

So, each one of the entry level property strategies has to be something that causes you the least amount of pain. I've had a lot of people in my network come to me through picking a strategy that just didn't fit in with their lifestyle. Think: it's time and it's energy, so it's got to align with your time and energy compacity.

How do I get the properties I want?

If you want to be building a portfolio that's going to replace your income, for example, there are a few ways of doing that. You can go down the single, vanilla buy-to-let route, which is a nice safe one, but you're going to need some cash to start up. Or you're going to end up doing some higher cash flow strategies, like HMOs or perhaps Supported Living. To get hold of these you're going to either need to be a property sourcer or make some good relationships with some very good property sourcers who will help you.

If you've got some cash there is no reason you can't buy a portfolio in one transaction and then you've got everything you want. If you are at a situation where you don't have any money, the most important thing is to invest in your time in your estate agency relationships, because if you don't have the money to pay a property sourcer, you can work with agents. It is going to take much more time, and trust building those relationships, but it's something that I would invest in if I was starting again – I'd be investing in the estate agency relationships.

What kind of money do I need to get my first property?

If you're on a rent-to-rent strategy I would say you probably only need about £3,000, to cover a few basics, such as the compliance stuff required as well as a modest budget to do a light makeover to make the property a bit more attractive. I started with my first rent-to-rent, which was just a 2-bedroom flat that I rented for £700. I then rented it out per room including bills at £700, so £1,400. It made me a few hundred pounds a month, but it was a nice easy rent-to-rent and the people in there absolutely loved it. All I spent was my deposit and money to do it up.

You're going to have some money to put down as a deposit. Effectively you're renting, so I think I had to put down £1,000. I probably only spent about £1,000 on furnishings; it was only a small flat so that's another £1,000 and then I put aside about £1,000 maximum just to get my compliance stuff up and running. You won't need that much but it's good just to have some. So, £3,000 is probably what you need to get your first property.

How can I find people I can trust to give me the right guidance?

Recommendations. Always. Don't go on what other people say about themselves. Go on what other people say about them. This is a very small incestuous world; you don't have to go too far to find out about a person. Make sure you get a good, rounded view. My mistake was that I got involved with people very, very quickly, that were way above me in terms of business and I thought the due diligence on them was just how successful they were online and that is not appropriate – you really do need to get to know a person. Don't go in too fast – just go slowly and get recommendations from people that they've worked with.

12. Emerald Fisk

About Emerald

Emerald is a Property Investor, Finance Broker, and future helicopter pilot. She loves doing property deals, mainly semi-commercial and small blocks of flats. When Emerald is not doing deals, she loves keeping fit, doing Crossfit and enjoying being active outside.

Based	Gloucestershire
Investment location	Gloucestershrie
Strategies	BRR – BTL (Block of flats and mixed use)
Favourite sayings/ affirmations/mottos	You have to work hard enough to not have to work hard.
A key learning you would like to share with readers	You can do anything you set your mind to.

Age 31

Job (if in a job previously)

Personal Trainer.

Why did you leave your job?

Wanted more freedom.

What do you love about your life now?

The variety.

Favourite books

- Robert T Kiyosaki, *Rich Dad, Poor Dad*
- Dale Carneigie, *How to Win Friends and Influence People*
- Denise Duffield Thomas, *Get Rich, Lucky Bitch*

Contact details

Email: emeraldfisk@hotmail.com

Emerald's Answers

How do I choose the right education, training and learning for me?

That's a really hard question. I don't know, really – how do you learn? You've got to read some books but you can't get everything from a book and, actually, you need to network with people and watch other people do it. When you watch your peers get going, you believe you can do it because they sat the same training as you.

For me it's getting yourself to training events, with people that can prove they have done it – not the sharks in the industry but the real deal. If you go and get that training in your chosen strategy, and you chose your strategy with your time available, with your area available, with your ability or belief of what you can make available. Then find a strategy, go to the events there, and eventually if you keep going back, you'll find yourself in a different position.

What happens when I start learning and realise there's more I don't know than I do know, or that there's too much to learn?

Don't worry about it. It's like thinking about the universe and you think, 'is there another Earth out there' and all this other stuff – don't worry about it. Just take some daily actions and forget about the rest.

How can I use my thoughts to help me do what I want?

Turn your thoughts into actions and then you'll do what you want to do, or get where you want to be.

How do I know which people to connect with to help me?

Well, it's like picking your friends at school – you just pick people you like and hopefully you get to the position where you can trust them, because we don't go to networking meetings just to meet people and hope they can help us. We go to networking meetings to meet good people and hope we can help them. If you go with that attitude, the right people will find you.

Is free help real help for me?

Sometimes with free help its really good and it's the right advice, but because you've not paid for it you're not so invested in it. So, maybe you don't take the advice, because it hasn't created pain for you to get it. But when you take paid advice, you've paid for that, so you are more likely to implement the advice you have been given. That's just because the part of giving someone money and not doing the thing you have paid for is enough to motivate most people. But there is nothing wrong with free advice.

How shall I prepare for opportunities?

Network with the right people. If a good opportunity comes along, you're surrounded by people who can make that opportunity happen. Get educated, believe in yourself, grow your confidence, grow your knowledge and when the opportunity comes along, you will make it work.

Which beginners' property books would you recommend?

The following, all by Rob Moore and Mark Homer:

- *Beginners' Property Secrets,*
- *Multiple Streams of Property income,*
- *The 44 Most Guarded Property Secrets*

Which property strategy should I follow?

I don't know. Which property strategy do you enjoy? Pick something you really enjoy doing, that works within your time restraints. But do whatever you enjoy – that will be the top tip.

THE 1ST PLACE.

How do I get the properties I want?

Talk to the owners. Find out if they have a problem and solve it – maybe by obtaining the property or by networking with people who want to acquire similar properties and raise finance for them.

What kind of money do I need to get my first property?

None. You can raise it all from investors, including the course fees, legal fees, every fee you can imagine – you can raise the finance for that if you believe you can.

How can I find people I can trust to give me the right guidance?

Network with people until you get to know them, and you'll know if you can trust them or not. In the same way you chat to people when you are out and about or in the same way you made friends at school, you find your people in any sort of network so just go out there and be you.

13. Fiona Crossley

About Fiona

I've created my dream life through my thoughts and feelings. Anyone can learn to do this too. Freedom is one of my highest values. My mission is to help at least a billion people feel good, loved and accepted. I want to help them grow into healthier, happier people. It's important to do what you love, be inspired, create, grow and be kind. Then, happiness and feeling good follows. Believe in the unseen world and have faith. Hard times make your stronger. 'Keep going' is my advice to you. It's worked for me!

Based	York
Investment location	Yorkshire
Strategies	BRRR – Buy, Refurbish, Rent, Refinance SA – Serviced Accommodation HMO – House of Multiple Occupancy
Favourite sayings/ affirmations/mottos	• Your brain is the boss • Aim high • Live life
Three key learnings you would like to share with readers	• You become what you think and feel • Invest in yourself and keep learning. • You can create your dream life. Believe!

Age 41

Job (if in a job previously)

Property investor from 18.

Why did you leave your job?

N/A

What do you love about your life now?

I have my dream life, health, wealth and happiness.

Education, training, learning

Continuous learning from books, audible, mentors and courses.

Favourite books

- Napoleon Hill, *Think and Grow Rich*
- Bob Proctor, *Change your Paradigm, Change Your Life*
- Deepak Chopra, *Seven Spiritual Laws of Success*

Contact details

Website: www.crossleypropertysolutions.co.uk

THE 1ST PLACE.

Email: Fiona@crossleypropertysolutions.co.uk

Fiona's Answers

How do I choose the right education, training and learning for me?

Go online and research training companies. Attend some free taster sections, which they will offer and then try another one, and then potentially another one. Pick the one that you feel the most comfortable with, that you think you'll get the most value out of and that have people that you connect with the most.

What happens when I start learning and realise there's more I don't know than I do know, or that there's too much to learn?

Accept that there are always things to learn in life. Accept that you're always learning every day and that you *should* be learning – you'll never know it all.

How can I use my thoughts to help me do what I want?

Your brain is the boss. Think about the things that you want to do, not the things that you don't want to do. You must always aim high and think of the things you want to achieve in life.

How do I know which people to connect with to help me?

Go to experienced people who have already done the things that you want to do.

Is free help real help for me?

In property training, I would go with paid training not free training.

How shall I prepare for opportunities?

Believe that there are opportunities everywhere. Open your eyes to people coming into your life and things coming into your life. There is opportunity everywhere, you just have to believe that there is.

Which beginners' property books would you recommend?

I'd recommend the *Progressive Property* books and research Rob Moore and Mark Homer's property beginner books too.

Which property strategy should I follow?

If you have no money to start off with, I'd go into No Money Down strategies. If you have some investment already, I'd start off with buy-to-let.

How do I get the properties I want?

You must talk to the estate agents and letting agents in the area. You need to tell everybody what you do, and properties will come to you through your network. You have to do a lot of viewings, a lot of talking, a lot of asking questions and go for the houses in your area to begin with.

What kind of money do I need to get my first property?

Realistically to buy your first property you need £5,000 for all of your legals, brokers and buying costs. Depending on the price of the property you'll need a deposit (if you're going to buy that house with a mortgage), so depending on what the price of the house was you're going to need a 20–25% deposit, plus buying costs.

How can I find people I can trust to give me the right guidance?

Go to training companies that offer training that has already led to successful results.

14. Halstead Ottley

About Halsted

Halstead has been investing in property for over 30 years. He started off buying single lets, then added HMOs and Serviced Accommodation properties to his portfolio. He invests in both residential and commercial buildings with the aim of bringing them into the residential world.

Halstead started his working life in retail with Ipswich Co-op as a trainee manager where he went off to college to learn his trade. As well as working hard to climb the corporate ladder, he was building and growing his property portfolio. Halstead believes in getting yourself educated no matter what field you're going into, and property was no exception.

He has trained under some of the best in the property industry, gaining knowledge for almost every aspect of property investing. When he's not doing property, he fulfils his passion as a Personal Trainer by working with individuals, groups and charities to help them reach their health goals.

Based	Ipswich
Investment location	East Coast
Strategies	B2L, HMO, SA, CC
Favourite sayings/ affirmations/mottos	• If it's to be, it's up to me
Three key learnings you would like to share with readers	• Action kills fear • Always have a minimum of two exits on a property deal • Learn to master your inner voice

Age 60

Job (if in a job previously)

Store Manager with Ipswich Co-op.

Why did you leave your job?

Didn't want to work late nights and Sundays.

What do you love about your life now?

Eating out with my family.

Education, training, learning

Here are some of the courses I've attended with 'Rich Dad' Rick Otton and Progressive Property: Buy to let, HMO, Commercial Conversion, Serviced Accommodation, Lease Options, Various Masterminds, Deal Packaging, Creative Finance, Expert Speaker.

Favourite books

- George S. Clason, *Richest Man in Babylon*
- Tom Grover, *Relentless*
- Shawn Steven, *Eat Smarter*

Contact details

Website: www.halsteadottley.com

Email: halsteadottley@progressivepropertynetwork.co.uk

Halstead's Answers

How do I choose the right education, training and learning for me?

Decide what your goal is and what it is that you want to achieve – is it cash flow, is it lump sums of money? Once you know what you want to achieve, find the strategy that will give you that. If you want lump sums, then it might be that you want to do flips and conversions. If it's cash flow you want, it might be that you do buy-to-lets and HMOs. Once you've decided that, then you pick what you're going to do first and get the education on that one.

What happens when I start learning and realise there's more I don't know than I do know, or that there's too much to learn?

I think that's a great place to be, because you never want to feel that you've learnt everything – if you do, I think you're just deluding yourself. It's great that you're on this continuous journey and I think that if you're going to do this you want to be constantly learning.

How can I use my thoughts to help me do what I want?

That self-talk in your head can either hold you back or help you move forwards. If you're having thoughts that might be holding you back, then it could be that you need to read, or listen, to something to help you overcome those and give you more of a positive insight into how to feed your brain. The world is full of negative things, so sometimes you have to balance that by putting something positive in.

How do I know which people to connect with to help me?

Everyone's got their own sort of moral compass and you're going to know the sort of people you're attracted to. They will be people who have the same sort of goals and drive as you, and your gut will tell you that when you meet them.

Every time I don't listen to my gut, it comes back to bite me. So, when you're talking to someone and you get that feeling, 'yep this is a good person' or 'this is someone that I should avoid' listen to your gut feeling.

Is free help real help for me?

It depends on who's giving you the free help. If someone was coming to me and I was giving them free help, I'd say that would be great. But if it was Joe down the pub who has absolutely no idea about property investing, but is trying to give you some advice on something he knows nothing about, then that's not worth anything at all.

How shall I prepare for opportunities?

Gain as much knowledge as you can. I invest in my investment area, so I get to know as much about my investment area as I can. I know what areas to buy in and where not to buy. I know the prices of two bed houses and three bed houses. You've got to get yourself as prepared as you can, then you'll be ready for opportunities. I think Les Brown had a really good quote: "It's better to be prepared for an opportunity and not have one, than to have an opportunity and not be prepared."

Which beginners' property books would you recommend?

Progressive have written some quite good ones and also *Property Magic* is quite a good book to read.

Which property strategy should I follow?

It depends on your goal and depends on what it is you want to achieve. I don't believe there's one size that fits all. That being said, if you're an absolute beginner, I suggest that you start with buy-to-lets so you get an idea of how property works. It might be that you buy one or two and then you can move on to a strategy that you know will fulfil whatever your goal is.

How do I get the properties I want?

You need to come at this with at least six to eight ways to find properties. Everybody knows at least one – which is to go off and see estate agents. But there are loads of different ways to find properties, like doing leaflets. If leaflets aren't working, it might be that you go to auctions. You just need to find loads and loads of different ways to bring properties to your funnel.

What kind of money do I need to get my first property?

That depends on your area. If the properties are around £200,000, obviously you're going to need 25% plus the stamp duty, plus the legal fees and any refurb costs. You'll be able to work out roughly what you need to start, but whatever number you come up with you need to add maybe 20% to that. There's always going to be things that come up that you hadn't accounted for.

How can I find people I can trust to give me the right guidance?

You go to networking groups, and you get recommendations. You meet people and you'll get that gut feeling, but also they may recommend you. Talk to people who are investing in the area, discuss other people, name names. Ask if they're doing much, ask about other people – the thing is, people will talk about you in a good light if that's the way you've come across. I think by going to different networking groups you'll find the right people.

15. Harvey

About Harvey

Harvey is the founder of Growth Properties Group, a small group of companies. His WHY is to live on his terms, and his mission is to help as many people live on their terms using property as a vehicle, through education, portfolio building and property management. He built his property portfolio and businesses in the Northeast of England, whilst living in the south, allowing him to spend time with his family and travel regularly. Having built up the systems and team to run from his phone, and largely on autopilot, he is now focused on helping others excel on their property journeys and build a remote investment lifestyle for themselves.

Based	Brentwood, Essex
Investment location	Stockton on Tees (NE England, UK)
Strategies	RBRR (Remote-buy, Refurbish, Refinance)
Favourite sayings/ affirmations/mottos	• Evolve your ideas • Live on your terms
Three key learnings you would like to share with readers	• You must have patience and engage in consistent action. • It's about progress not perfection. • We all have different skills, why, time, money and desires – find what works for you not what works for somebody else.

Age 44

Job (if in a job previously)

Full-time property / business / coach

What do you love about your life now?

Living on my terms.

Education, training, learning?

Left school with not one GCSE or any formal qualifications, and am a little dyslexic.

Favourite books

- George S. Clason, *The Richest Man in Babylon*
- Mel Robbins, *The 5 Second Rule*

Contact details

Website: www.remotepropertyinvestor.co.uk

Harvey's Answers

How do I choose the right education, training and learning for me?

It depends what you want to achieve and where you are, and it depends on how you prefer to learn. Everyone has a different way of learning, some people can just take some videos and run with it, some people just read a book and run with it. You really have got to know yourself.

For me, I find it's good if you get some accountability and not in one form, such as if you are part of some sort Mastermind group, something you continuously go back and have group accountability, group inspiration and a little bit of over a period of time.

What happens when I start learning and realise there's more I don't know than I do know, or that there's too much to learn?

You have got to zoom back out and just be realistic. There is always going to be more to learn. You've really got to zoom out and be realistic in the steps you've got to take – focus on your steps as opposed to your end goal. So many people talk about manifestation, law of attraction and things like this, and too many people focus on what the end is instead of what they've got to do along the way. So just zoom out and focus on what your next actionable steps are instead of the end stuff, and just keep chunking at them.

How can I use my thoughts to help me do what I want?

So, we have about 75,000 thoughts per day and unfortunately only about 9% percent of those are original thoughts, they're repeated stuff, so unless you want what you had yesterday tomorrow, you've got to learn how to change your thought process.

A quick hack on changing your thought process, especially if you're stuck in a negative loop is a 5-second rule. Look up a lady called Mel Robins, who says that our thought processes are auto pilot – they're not done consciously. As soon you catch yourself having a negative thought process, say 5,4,3,2,1 and interrupt the pattern. Some people use an elastic band on their wrist, so as soon as you realise you are having that thought process snap the band, so you're just constantly training your thoughts away from that negativity. Then start thinking about the stuff that you know is more positive and that is going to drive you forward as opposed to the negative internal thoughts that we all get, by the way, but some people control it better than others.

How do I know which people to connect with to help me?

Social media is fantastic for this today. There are online CVs at the moment, where you can check people out and see a little bit out there. But there is a lot of BS also. Some people paint a picture which is not actually so true. You can speed this process up if you do this strategically, but you just got to get out there and kiss some frogs, unfortunately.

Get around people and look at it like a development exercise, just figuring people out. BUT... yes, social media helps speed that up without question. You can see what they are doing, what they've done but you've just got to get out there and do it and recognise if they are a fit or not.

Is free help real help for me?

It can be to a degree, and it depends on the person. I've got tons of free help which has been absolutely amazing, but I get massive momentum from paying for help as well, because I just pay attention.

How shall I prepare for opportunities?

I think it links a little bit back to your thought process, you know. You just got to keep that mind really open with what you do. The biggest thing that is going to hold us back from opportunity is that internal dialogue, so the more that you can train your mind around to having the right thought process the more you are going to have an open mind to opportunities.

There is a fantastic book by Shawn Actor called *Happiness Advantage*, and it shows the psychology and science behind positive psychology. The reason people with positive psychology are more successful is because their mind gravitates to solutions rather than problems, and it sees opportunity a hell of a lot quicker as a result. So, if you can get your mindset right and study positive psychology – and I don't mean the BS positive psychology, telling yourself that you are rich and happy when you blatantly know you're not – but if you get that psychology done correctly then it's going to drive you forward for opportunity.

Which beginners' property books would you recommend?

I really like David Tarn's book, *The Complete No-Nonsense Guide to Becoming A UK Property Investor: The 123 on Property Investing*. I think it's really, really good start up book.

Which property strategy should I follow?

Again, it goes back to, 'Depends where you are'. If you are already a builder you could probably jump up a little bit further ahead in your strategy. I think, if you're a beginner, most people (but not everybody, to be really clear) should start on single let properties to just cut your teeth.

Get used to dealing with a builder, to costing a refurb, to dealing with a letting agent or or managing a tenant yourself. If you're a builder or surveyor, maybe you know how to do refurbs already so you might be able to jump a little bit higher up. Or you might have some experience previously in managing properties, you might have worked in an estate agent and managed tenants. So, it depends where your start point is but in most cases I would encourage you to cut your teeth on something simpler first before jumping up.

How do I get the properties I want?

Persistent action really. Be realistic where you are going to start but get started. And if you want to be doing developments and you've never done developments before or even costed a refurb before, you've got to just work your way up that ladder, but you've got to be taking consistent action to work towards where you want to be.

What kind of money do I need to get my first property?

Depends on the strategy. If you start off on the simplest strategy, probably you can get into it for £20–£30K: the simplistic BRR, light refurb for around £10K and around £15K deposit. I think that will get most people started if you are very resourceful.

The unfortunate thing is, if you've got no experience, most people don't want to lend you money unless you've got family members who can help. You can do it with other people's money, but the reality is it's not so common unless you've got transferable skills to offer. It can be done but it takes a hell of a lot more effort if you haven't got that.

How can I find people I can trust to give me the right guidance?

You want to have a good front end Qualified/Disqualified process for people. And remember that the power of your questions is the power of results. So, you really want to have different sorts of people to build into your network. And you want to think and create the sort of questions that you can ask them and interview them with.

It's not an official interview, but take people on using an interview process – and the better questions you are going to ask them, the quicker you are going to identify the right people, but it's going to take a little bit of trial and error and the kissing of a few frogs. Instead of giving a frog maybe a long lingering French kiss you might do a peck on the cheek – but you do have to trial and error a bit, to build an outer networking around you.

16. Hazel de Kloe

About Hazel

Having started her professional life as a musician and music teacher, Hazel then went on to build a multi-million-pound property portfolio, together with her husband, and became financially free in 2011. Since then, she set up Why Property Works, a coaching and mentoring business to help others achieve the same. More recently, she has co-founded The Freedom Club, a platform to facilitate financial empowerment and enable even more people to live life on their own terms.

Based	Hythe, Kent
Investment location	South Wales, Milton Keynes, Sheffield, South Coast, London
Strategies	BTL and HMO, some development and flip, and holiday lets
Favourite sayings/ affirmations/mottos	• You don't have to get it right, you just have to get it going! • You don't just go into business, you grow into business
Three key learnings you would like to share with readers	• Make sure you are 'lit up' by thinking about going into property, otherwise you're going to find it tough • Find out what you need to in order to get going, but don't be caught up in 'analysis paralysis' • Find out what you can give and how you can help people in order to do really well... this is a people business

Age 48

Job (if in a job previously)

Musician and music teacher.

Why did you leave your job?

I had a problem with my jaw, which was quite debilitating for my profession and also we had built up our property business enough for me to stop at this time.

What do you love about your life now?

The freedom and time to do what I want, with who I want, when I want, within the usual family commitments and responsibilities. Living by the sea, and also having the ability to home educate our son, who is now 14 and running his own business.

Education, training, learning

Have studied many personal development materials over the years. I particularly like T Harv Eker, Anthony Robbins and Eckhart Tolle. We went through the Whitney training programme when we first started out, which was useful. We have had various mentors over the years who have also helped us in different areas of life and business.

Favourite books

- Bob Burg & John David Mann, *The Go Giver*

THE 1ST PLACE.

- Ekhart Tolle, *The Power Of Now*
- T Harv Eker, *Secrets of the Millionaire Mind*

Contact details

Website: www.the-freedom-club.com; www.whypropertyworks.co.uk

Email: hazel@whypropertyworks.co.uk

Hazel's Answers

How do I choose the right education, training and learning for me?

It's the same as choosing the right mentor. You've got to expose yourself to a wide variety of books, podcasts, e-books and other free training. Take on board different people's opinions and see what resonates most with you. Don't just go with an organisation because they're promising you the earth. You've got to go with what sits, feels and sounds right and resonates with you – someone who's inspiring, but you can see the practical steps that you have to take in order to get there.

What happens when I start learning and realise there's more I don't know than I do know, or that there's too much to learn?

Part of the nature of the beast is that you're going to feel overwhelmed when you first start out. However far you are down the road you'll still feel like you're learning. You work over it, round it, under it you basically get through it, and you seek advice from the right people. You're always going to feel that there's more to know, more to learn, because it is an ever-evolving process. Most important is to just get going, and you will work it out along the way.

How can I use my thoughts to help me do what I want?

Your journey absolutely starts in the head. There are some great mindset coaches out there – people like Anthony Robbins and Joe Dispenza. Remember that Henry Ford phrase, 'if you believe you can or believe you can't, you're right.' It's a question of what you feed your mind. Become aware of the negative, fearful or anxious thoughts, that's half the battle.

Then, slowly but surely replace them with positive ones. It's constantly weeding your mind garden from negative things, thanking them for sharing and then starting to feed your mind the more conscious, positive things that you know. Tell yourself you're not perfect, you know you don't know everything, but you're on the right track and you'll start to emanate this sense of belief and confidence. Half the battle is believing that you can do it.

How do I know which people to connect with to help me?

Anyone who's sharing good quality stuff that resonates with you is a good person to connect with – whether on a macro scale, like podcasts and books, or a micro level by meeting with them at a networking event or having a business meeting. You don't know, what you don't know, so use Google if you're looking at working with someone, whoever they are. Find out what other people are saying about them, get an understanding of their reputation and whether they're aligned with what they're saying so you can trust what they say. Listen to your gut instinct – you've got to have a good gut feeling in this business, both in the sense of who you're working with and what property deals you're doing.

Is free help real help for me?

It can be, yes. People who are worth their salt will be happy to give away really useful tips – they know what they're doing, they care about other people and will give some great free advice. Equally there are people out there who will give you free advice because they have an agenda, so find out what that agenda is before you follow them.

How shall I prepare for opportunities?

Explore and set up your finances and strategy. Understand the numbers and the mechanics of how deals are set up and how they work financially, so you'll know when you've got a good deal. Don't think you have to be a maths genius to understand it, but understanding the finances has a huge part to play.

Which beginners' property books would you recommend?

My property book, *Why Property Works* is ideal for beginners.

Which property strategy should I follow?

It's dependent on the goal you're trying to achieve – whether it's cash flow, capital growth or a mixture of the two. You have to understand that strategy, whether you're going to own the properties yourself, or whether you're becoming the middle person, like an agent. Understanding the strategy helps you achieve your ultimate goal and will determine what types of properties you're going to get involved in.

How do I get the properties I want?

Start with an idea of what's going to work for you, which areas are going to work best for you for the strategy that you want to adopt, and then drill down to the property types within those areas. Then, gain more understanding of the micro aspects of those individual areas. My course cover all of this!

What kind of money do I need to get my first property?

This is dependent on the type of strategy and the area that you're working with. That's why it's important to understand your budget first and what you have to work with. If you're starting off with nothing, then you're going to have to work very differently compared to having thousands sitting in the bank. You have to grow into this business and start out with that mindset expansion. If you have a decent amount of cash, then just be aware of locking money into deposits. Ideally you want to work on retrieving money back out by buying correctly and adding value. Working with JV partners can be a good idea if you don't have funds, but you have to work responsibly with those funds. You'll have to learn a lot before even considering this path.

How can I find people I can trust to give me the right guidance?

It's finding and having that alignment. Do some Google searches on people, do your due diligence and research the people that you're thinking about working with, then go with your gut feeling.

17. Jack Dawhra

About Jack

Jack started his career in the family export business at the age of 14 and moved on to start his own business after a few years. After running several businesses and investments for many years, Jack now manages a portfolio of investment properties, which he started in 2003, and is actively involved in property development projects.

At the age of 25, Jack was depressed and suicidal and his businesses and health were suffering, but he picked himself up and started educating himself. He went on to study BA (Hons) Leadership & Management, Finance (Diploma) and Consultancy (Diploma) and has read several hundred books on leadership and management. He also reads widely – books on Neuro-linguistic programming (NLP), spirituality and biographies of influential people.

For many years, Jack has worked with property, tech, fashion, retail, finance, transportation, personal development and online businesses. Now he invests most of his time building the Property Tech Platform called PEN, helping property investors expand their portfolio and power teams, and is involved in property development and property finance. PEN is the world's first property social platform. Jack also has his own YouTube channel and helps entrepreneurs create powerful businesses and sell them for life-changing amounts.

Based	Slough, UK
Investment location	London and Blackpool
Strategies	Planning uplifts and hotels
Favourite sayings/ affirmations/mottos	'Remembering that you are going to die is the best way I know to avoid the trap of thinking you have something to lose. You are already naked. There is no reason not to follow your heart.' Steve Jobs
Three key learnings you would like to share with readers	• Have a big grand vision and work smart towards it. • Humility is the most important ingredient of success. • Personal and professional development plays the biggest part.

Age 42

Job (if in a job previously)

Jack has been running businesses for the past 27 years and has substantial experience in leading businesses and investments. He continues to do this.

What do you love about your life now?

Everything.

Education, training, learning

See about me.

Favourite books

Anything by Dr Wayne Dyer.

Contact details

Websties:www.propertyentrepreneursnetwork.com/site/signup, jackdawhra.com/

Email: Ask@propertyentrepreneursnetwork.com

Jack's Answers

How do I choose the right education, training and learning for me?

Look at the value you're paying for your training and mentoring. Let's say you're thinking of investing £3,000 for a 3-day training course – just slow down a minute. You're going to pay £1,000 for a single day – that's over £120 per hour. And I see a lot of training programs out there that charge a lot more even than that.

Ask yourself if it's worth it. My answer in most cases is NO**,** because some of these trainers have only been in business for ten years. If, say, if I was paying £5,000 or £10,000 to shadow maybe Richard Branson or Elon Musk it might be worth it, but if you're paying a trainer that's making money most of their money from trainings and mentoring, you got to slow down and think, 'Is it worth paying £1,000 a day?'

When you have learnt all of the free stuff, then decide if it's worth paying for more. So, if someone, like myself, has done a podcast or created free YouTube videos, go and listen / watch all of those before approaching them for paid training.

That will give you a clue as to the value, and always look at this in terms of return on investment. It's a logical decision, if you're investing £10,000, can you make 20, 30, 50 at the back of that? If the answer is NO, please don't invest. If the answer is YES, please do.

Most mentors who charge will be able to, in most cases, tell you that if you're going to invest £10,000 in my mentoring program the likelihood of you making that £10,000 is very high. I tell people when they're speaking with me, '*If you invest in my program, I promise you that if you take action, you will make that money a million-fold over, not two times over, three times over, but if you don't take action, with due respect, you might as well just not take this mentoring program*'.

What happens when I start learning and realise there's more I don't know than I do know, or that there's too much to learn?

One thing I always share with people is, 'The more you learn, the more you realise that you don't know how much you don't know'. It's just one of those learning experiences, it's almost like you're diving into something that has no end to it. Learning has no end to it; the more you learn, the more humble you become, the more humility there is the more you realise you don't know AND the more it makes you humble, and so on and so forth.

But it's not about how much you've got to learn – it's about how much you know and can apply and make money.

How can I use my thoughts to help me do what I want?

You can. If you want to do something, you go and do it. There's a saying, 'If you think about something more than a certain number of seconds, you'll find excuses not to do it', and every single person I've met in my life who is successful has only been successful because of fast decision making.

THE 1ST PLACE.

As long as you have 70% of the information needed to make the decision you are about to make, you must take it now and not wait. OK, so it's not the thinking, it's actually in the doing! As long as you have 70% of the information, take a decision and go and do it.

How do I know which people to connect with to help me?

Good question. One of the most important skills as an entrepreneur is to learn how to assess people – not judge, but assess people, and that comes with experience and learning to be able to see through the words that have been used in communication. Ask yourself, what is it they're sharing, what is it they're not sharing? It's the body language and the tone.

Over a sustained period of time, the more you practice the more you learn to assess people and the better you become at it. It's a vital skill, because you only want to work with people who are authentic.

Is free help real help for me?

Yes, and I'll tell you why. Let's say someone is giving out their books for free, or maybe for £5 or £10. They've put all their life experience into that book so that's not a lot of money and is actually free help, so it is helpful. At the same time, if somebody is giving a free session you've got nothing to lose – go and take that session and decide at the end of it if it's worthwhile you investing any further. Always take it. Sometimes it may not be worth it, sometimes it is – you have to take your chances.

How shall I prepare for opportunities?

Put your head down. In 2009 or maybe 2010, I actually disappeared for six months from my circle of friends, my family, everyone. All I did was learning, learning, learning, learning, learning, and I wanted to sort a few things that were not right in my life. I wanted to put them right. That's how long it took me, took me – six months to put many of those things right. So, sharpen your focus and get the work done.

Which beginners' property books would you recommend?

- Simon Zutshi, *Property Magic*
- Rob Moore, *44 Property Secrets* and *Multiple Streams of Property Income*
- Lloyd Girardi, *Property Development: Discover the Secrets to Becoming a Property Developer; from Scratch, Using None of Your Own Money*

Which property strategy should I follow?

Depends on where you are in your journey and how much money you have. If, let's say, you have very little money, it may be good to start with rent-to-rent. Don't start with sourcing, as a lot of trainers teach it. It's not the best strategy to focus on. Sourcing can be a side hustle, but start with rent to rent and make sure you choose the right location. If you don't actually live in the right location, choose somewhere maybe half an hour, an hour's drive away, but make sure you focus on one location and one strategy.

If you have over £100,000, Buy, Refurbish, Refinance (BRR) is a great strategy. If you have more than that, then maybe conversions and developments. If you have more than that, maybe even land developments. If you are anywhere in the middle even leasing hotels is a great strategy, as are option deals, lease options – all of those are great strategies as long as you have a little bit of money around.

How do I get the properties I want?

What do you want in the first place? I think most people struggle with this. When you ask people this question, and most people cannot even answer. So, what do you want?

If you want to find the right properties, I think one of the biggest challenges most people face is finding the deals that are healthy and stack up well. It's a hell of a skill you're not going to learn this in a month or two. Find yourself a trainer or mentor who will teach you how to find the right deals.

I mean I can walk down the street find you a deal in ten minutes because it's like when you have a situation where you didn't know about something and then you come across it and now you see it everywhere – and that's because it was not on your conscious level before, but now that it is, you see that opportunity everywhere. Same applies to opportunities –when you learn where to spot them and bring them to your conscious level, you'll see them everywhere and this comes with training and mentoring.

What kind of money do I need to get my first property?

Depends on where you are. If you're in Central London, you're talking about millions, if you are in the Greater London area you could get away with £100,000 or even less, and if you're up North you could buy very large properties, even hotels, for very little money.

Do always make sure that the return on an investment is good, I think a lot of people invest into strategies where they only make like 5–10%. I would normally look at 100% return on an investment in a year. There are deals like that available – where you can make 100% return on investment – as long as you know where to look, you just need to have the right know how.

How can I find people I can trust to give me the right guidance?

Ok, again this is a life skill. It takes time to learn and assess people. Also, surround yourself with people who are creative and high achievers because it's the creative people who will bring something new into this world. For example, even in the property industry if you look at someone and they are maybe adding one or two properties a year to their portfolio, surround yourself with this person, because they have learnt a skill that you can maybe just observe and learn yourself. Maybe you can approach them and offer to work for them for a couple of weeks to shadow them. Many people will say yes to that.

18. James Doran

About James

James is a dad to three little girls, property investor and developer in the north east of England. He took a leap of faith out of offshore life to go full-time in his property business.

He now helps people invest in property with a hands-free investment service, building their property portfolios and providing development opportunities. James also has his own YouTube channel.

Based	Newcastle
Investment location	North East England
Strategies	Property Sourcing, BTL, Buy to Flip, Serviced Accommodation
Favourite sayings/ affirmations/mottos	Life happens for you and not to you
Three key learnings you would like to share with readers	• Surround yourself with the right people, build a great network • The challenges you will face are what shapes you, embrace them all and find a way past them • Get awareness of your self-talk and weed out any negative chat – it's all an inner game

Age 43

Job (if in a job previously)

Offshore worker

Why did you leave your job?

I was away from home too much with my offshore work and wanted to be home full-time with my three girls.

What do you love about your life now?

I love having the freedom to set my own schedule, to create the life I want for myself and my girls.

Education, training, learning

- Paul McFadden, *Property Protégé*
- Paul McFadden, *Platinum Inner Circle*

Favourite books

- Napoleon Hill, *Think and Grow Rich*
- Maxwell Maltz, *Psycho-Cybernetics*
- Brendan Burchard *High Performance Habits*

Contact details

Website: www.tynesidepropertyinvestments.com

Linktree: https://linktr.ee/Jamesdoran1

Email: info@tynesidepropertyinvestments.com

James' Answers

How do I choose the right education, training and learning for me?

You've got to choose someone that you resonate with. Make sure you follow them online, follow them on social media, see how they perform and see how they come across. Maybe do a little digging into their background, find out where they started and how they got to where they are in property. Also, speak to other people who have had mentorship from them and see how they found it and see if they are getting results.

What happens when I start learning and realise there's more I don't know than I do know, or that there's too much to learn?

There's always more to learn than you know. That's just the way it is. 'You don't know what you don't know,' as they say. You never stop learning. You've just got to understand that this applies to life in general, not just property. Learning is non-stop and if you feel there's too much to learn, or maybe you're feeling a bit overwhelmed, then you need to refocus. Dial into what you're looking to achieve and just focus on that until you get it mastered, before moving onto something else.

How can I use my thoughts to help me do what I want?

Get control of them to start with. Awareness of your own internal dialogue is absolutely key. Your thoughts control your actions, so you need to be aware of what kind of thoughts you're having – whether they be positive, negative, doubtful. You need to be clear on what your mind is telling you.

Your mind has a habit of telling you things to keep you safe, but that's not always in your best interests. If you're looking to achieve certain things in life that you've never achieved before, it's going to be uncomfortable, and your mind will often try to stop you stretching your comfort zone and taking risks. But, we need to take risks in the property game, or any game, in order to progress, and your mind is going to try and talk you out of it. It's so important to be aware of that and be prepared for it.

How do I know which people to connect with to help me?

Get out there and network as much as possible. Go to property events, business events, all kinds of networking events. Once you've decided your strategy and what you're looking to achieve, then you know which people you're going to need around you, whether they're solicitors, builders, finance brokers, investors. It's all about networking, getting out there and meeting as many people as possible. You need to grow your network from day one.

Is free help real help for me?

Yes, why not? I wouldn't down-value it, just because it's free. Saying that though, if you're paying for help, like mentorship and consultations, then that can have the added bonus of 'well, I paid for it, so I'm going to take action on it, rather than waste that money'. But free help has definitely got its value, as long as you're taking action on it and it's the right action for you.

How shall I prepare for opportunities?

You get ready for them. Just keep your eyes open. Opportunities come when you set your goals. When you set whatever goal it is you're looking to achieve, your mind will start to search for ways to achieve that goal. We have this thing in our brain known as your Reticular Activating System (RAS). It filters the world around you and helps direct you towards those goals.

For example, when it comes to property deals – you'll see certain properties while you're driving down a street, that you may have driven down hundreds of times. Your eyes will automatically be drawn to properties that look like they could be a good development opportunity. You'll notice the property, make a note of it and take action. The property was always there, but your mind wasn't filtering for it previously, until you set your goals.

If somebody puts an opportunity in front of you, take action on that. Assess it first and make sure it's right for you. You're not going to say yes to every single opportunity, but you'll know some you should knock back. Have a quick look first, assess it and if it's something you want to move forward with, do that at the nearest possible time you can. Don't leave it too long – because there will be somebody else who will take the action and take that opportunity.

Which beginners' property books would you recommend?

Rich Dad Poor Dad is a great book for people starting out in property. It's one of the first books I read when I got started, and is great for putting things into perspective. The 'why' in property investing is so important.

Which property strategy should I follow?

It depends on what your goals are and where you're at – what resources you have available. Start small maybe with a buy-to-let property, which is pretty much entry level. There's generally progression from buy-to-lets to something more advanced like HMOs and then maybe on to Serviced Accommodation or Buy to Flip developments.

It all depends on what you're looking for and where you are financially. If you don't have any money, you might want to start with property sourcing and help other people find their own investment properties, until you've accrued enough funds to start investing yourself. You've got to assess where you're at and where you want to go, and how you'd like to do it because enjoying it is important too.

How do I get the properties I want?

You've got to go out and look for them. You can either go and look for them yourself or you can enlist the services of someone who goes out and finds properties such as a property sourcing agent.

What kind of money do I need to get my first property?

I'm going to say none. You can raise finance with investors to help get your first property. If you find the right property, then offer an investor a return on their money if they fund the deal, then technically you're buying the property no money down. You would probably look to structure the deal in a way that you would pay the investor back over X amount of years, with an agreed X amount of return on their investment until the property becomes yours out right.

How can I find people I can trust to give me the right guidance?

I would say start networking and start speaking to people. Your network is going to be there to support you and guide you throughout your property journey. If it's something specific you're needing guidance with, ask within your network. You'll get recommendations from people, and there's a good chance those being recommended are good to work with and can help you progress.

19. Jamie Madill

About Jamie

Jamie is a property investor and HMO developer. He specialises in working with investors, and his clients work with him because he is an active property developer. He has a significant property portfolio comprising of buy-to-let houses, flats and HMOs.

Jamie has written two books, *The Property Ironman* and *The HMO Blueprint*, and is the host of The HMO Experience podcast. Jamie is the founder of the PPN Property Network franchise, and hosted PPN St Pancras in London for many years. He also runs HMO courses and mentoring services for property investors and speaks at property events.

Based	Hertfordshire
Investment location	East Midlands and Yorkshire
Strategies	Buy-to-let, rent-to-rent and HMOs
Favourite sayings/ affirmations/mottos	• If my mind can conceive it, if my heart can believe it, then I can achieve it. • You define your own life. Don't let other people write your script • *If it is not right do not do it; if it is not true do not say it*
Three key learnings you would like to share with readers	• Don't believe the hype, always do your research. It takes years to make money but only a second to lose it. • If it was easy, everyone would be doing it. The key is to keep going. • Change is constant, so rather than wish it were different accept that it is pointless to fight against it. Learning to accept and adapt makes you more resilient.

Age 51

Job (if in a job previously)

Business Development Director, UK & EMEA, Thomson Reuters.

Why did you leave your job?

Commuting for 18 years and often missing my children's school plays, dance shows and family events due to working long hours was something I wasn't prepared to do any more.

THE 1ST PLACE.

What do you love about your life now?

I have more flexibility in what I do now, and I really enjoy seeing the results that my students and investors get – and the difference it makes to their lives.

Education, training, learning?

- This is a long list, but the brief overview is:
- Masters in Business Administration (MBA)
- Various property training on a number of different strategies
- Various business, property and personal development podcasts

Favourite books

- Mo Gawdat, *Solve for Happy*
- Darren Hardy, *The Compound Effect*
- Chris Voss, *Never Split the Difference*
- Malcolm Gladwell, *Outliers*

Contact details

Email: jamiemadillproperties@gmail.com

Jamie's Answers

How do I choose the right education, training and learning for me?

You identify what you want to achieve in property, you find the strategy that will help you get there, and you go and find the training company, resources or otherwise that delivers that. In terms of the best training, all the training is pretty much the same. All the property strategies are pretty much the same, but the deliverer and the people who deliver that are different. So maybe,

- it's people that not only are doing the business strategy you want to do, but have done it themselves so they have loads of case studies AND
- it's people that you resonate with

If you find people that tick both of these boxes, they are probably the best ones to go with.

What happens when I start learning and realise there's more I don't know than I do know, or that there's too much to learn?

You take it one step at a time, and realise that you're never going to learn everything, you're never going to know everything, you're never going to know every single answer to every single question. But you've got to get started, you've got to start implementing it step-by-step, whatever you are doing, and then you learn from experience over time. You'll never learn it all but there will be new opportunities, new experiences, new challenges, and new questions that happens all the time. That's just part and parcel of being a property investor, it will never change.

How can I use my thoughts to help me do what I want?

By putting those thoughts into action, otherwise they are just thoughts.

How do I know which people to connect with to help me?

Again, you identify what help you need; is it people in professional services, accountants, solicitors, etc? Is it trades, builders, carpenters, etc? Then you find people in your local vicinity or where you are looking to invest that can fulfil those tasks and give you the help that you need. Before you decide though, in any of these cases, I recommend you ask to speak to clients of theirs to get feedback and recommendations first.

Is free help real help for me?

Yes, it is, as long as it's answering the questions that you have. However, you must understand that free help will never give you all the answers or all the help that you need. It's a false economy, in my opinion, to spend lots of time getting free answers and free resources as opposed to investing in those resources and help.

How shall I prepare for opportunities?

I guess it depends on the context. So, if we are thinking about property opportunities, understanding what it is you are doing and the type of properties you are looking for helps you when opportunities come your way. Whether it be through agents or direct to vendor to owners or landlords, for example, knowing what a deal looks like or an opportunity looks like and what you're looking for is key. But I would also say that looking for opportunities in any aspect of life is just about being open and having conversations with people, because you never know what opportunities could come your way that you might never have even thought about.

Which beginners' property books would you recommend?

Property Beginners Secrets might be one, *Property Magic*, I think, is another. Again, it all depends on the strategy. If you want a general property book, there are a few books out there but if you want a book specifically about property for beginners, i.e. looking at a specific strategy, all I would do is go onto Amazon and type in your strategy and you'll have thousands of books to choose from. Then go with ones that have had good reviews, for example, and best sellers, then you can't go too far wrong.

Which property strategy should I follow?

I always believe you should think about the end before the beginning. So, what is it you want to achieve? Is it X amount of income, or Y amount of equity, or a combination of both? Depending on those answers, you simply look at the opportunities and property strategies that can help you get there, and be aware that what you want to achieve will probably change over time. So, why not set yourself a 12-month target of whatever it is you want to achieve and find a strategy to help you do that. Once you've got that target, once you've done that for a year, then you can reassess and maybe go again or even pin it to a different strategy, depending on what your next goal is.

How do I get the properties I want?

The first thing is to understand what it is you want; some people don't know. Some people want a property, but they are not very clear what that could be. So, again it comes back to the results. If you need, for example, £500 net income a month, in some areas of the country that could be a 1-bedroom flat but in other parts of the country it could be a 3-bedroom house. So, it all depends if you want to buy a flat or a house.

THE 1ST PLACE.

Then this is a different strategy to managing and controlling houses to get that income. You can typically find properties either by going directly to homeowners, whether they are landlords, commercial property owners or managed through agents.

What kind of money do I need to get my first property?

Again, it depends on your strategy. Are you looking to acquire your own properties or are you simply looking for income from other properties you can manage? Both can deliver and both are very different. So, if you are doing something like rent-to-rent or HMO, for example, you'll need a very small amount of money for the rent-to-rent compared to if you want to buy your first HMO, because that will need a deposit, legal fees, purchasing fees and potentially a refurb as well. So, it all depends on the strategy you want to follow, and this will determine the resources you'll need from the beginning.

How can I find people I can trust to give me the right guidance?

That is simple. Go on to social media groups and ask for recommendations, and once you get those recommendations – let's just say you have a handful of people – see if you can see the testimonials and results they've achieved.

20. Jane Bayler

About Jane

Known as The Smart Connector through her podcast, author, brand marketer and business growth expert, Jane helps experts to market themselves – stand out from the crowd and build online assets to explode their growth.

As a strategic marketer, she meets clients to create a bespoke plan for them. This may or may not include online courses, funnels, podcasts, scorecards, books, automated webinars, or live events. The plan is to increase their authority, credibility and visibility, so they can make the impact they want in the world.

Jane spent 20 years managing and developing business for global advertising and media agencies and creating campaigns for world-leading brands such as Coca-Cola, British Airways, ITV and Discovery Networks before scaling and selling a brand identity business to a US communications group. She brings the same skillset to her property work, connecting HNW investors with property development projects in the South East of England.

Based	London
Investment location	South East England
Strategies	Development Investing, Land Sourcing
Favourite sayings/ affirmations/mottos	Always be clear about your purpose or others will use you for theirs
Three key learnings you would like to share with readers	• Integrity first • Choose partners on the basis of character not results • Always verify claims

Age 60

Job (if in a job previously)

20 years in global marketing, MD of Futurebrand E&P (brand marketing and identity consultancy).

Why did you leave your job?

Sold the business.

What do you love about your life now?

Creative and professional freedom.

Education, training, learning

Drama/English Degree, Postgraduate Theatre Design, Extensive Professional Development including Millbank Land Academy and Progressive Success.

Favourite books

- Stephen R. Covey, *The 7 Habits of Highly Effective People*
- John Demartini, *The Values Factor*

THE 1ST PLACE.

- Greg Baier, *Real Love*

Contact details

Website: www.janebayler.com

Linktree: https://linktr.ee/JaneyB

Email: jane@janebayler.com

Jane's Answers

How do I choose the right education, training and learning for me?

I prefer one-to-one mentorship because that way you get a strategic focus on your business. However, that is going to be more expensive, so if you can't afford the one-to-one mentorship, then I would take a course, any kind of a course. Make sure you have the opportunity to get to know, and get some support from, people who are practitioners in your industry who aren't offering formal mentorships. Don't just rely on courses alone.

What happens when I start learning and realise there's more I don't know than I do know, or that there's too much to learn?

There's never too much to learn. I think anybody that's serious about building a good business has to commit to being a lifelong learner. Everybody, every winner was once a beginner. Accept the stage that you're at and know that things will get easier as time goes on, and as your learning increases.

How can I use my thoughts to help me do what I want?

It's very important that you program your brain to be a winner and not to accept defeat. Gratitude is very important because it stops you from feeling sorry for yourself which, together with self-pity, are saboteurs of success. Also use affirmations. These are declarations you can use to self-hypnotise in a way. Use certain kinds of statements that will prime and condition the brain for success. It doesn't mean you can't have difficult feelings, we all have difficult feelings, but it is important to prime and condition the brain I believe, and it is entirely possible to do that with certain techniques.

How do I know which people to connect with to help me?

The most important thing is their values and to find out whether they are a good person or not. The only way to do that is to observe their actions over time. People who are good people will go out of their way to help you, whether you're paying them or not. They won't be stupid commercially, but they will be good people and their interest in you will be in you as a person – as opposed to just being a source of money for them. Just look at their behaviour over time – don't jump in too quickly.

Is free help real help for me?

Yes, free help is real help, as long as it's from people who know what they're talking about. Unfortunately, there are a lot of people who will pretend to know what they're talking about because people get an ego boost, or some personal kudos from masquerading as experts when they're not. It is important to avoid those kinds of people and only listen to people who are seriously successful, if you're going to get free advice.

How shall I prepare for opportunities?

This comes down to priming and conditioning the brain first of all. If you believe that opportunities are everywhere, opportunities will be everywhere, if you believe that there are no deals to be had, there will be no deals to be had. So, you have to open your mind to possibility without pushing it, without trying to turn a deal that isn't a deal into a deal. You have to believe that there are opportunities out there all the time for us in property, and in business and in life.

Which beginners' property books would you recommend?

A property book I remember thinking was quite a good basic book was *Property Magic* by Simon Zutshi. I don't read many beginners' property books these days, but that one I thought was quite good.

Which property strategy should I follow?

It depends on you and your life. For me, I ended up putting together high net worth investors and developers because that was something that I could do working from home, and I'd done a bit of land sourcing. I ended up doing that because I had children and I didn't want to travel. For me, it was an emotional decision and a practical decision.

I chose a strategy that worked with my life – and the other reason why I chose it was because I like development. I'm very connected to it personally and so it really depends on your situation. I didn't want to be spending my time going around what I call skanky houses because they don't excite me. I'm a creator, a creative person.

How do I get the properties I want?

We probably all want to have a huge portfolio of immensely valuable properties as quickly as possible. Everybody wants the same thing to a certain extent, but again it comes back to being clear about what it is you're looking for in the short term.

What kind of money do I need to get my first property?

That depends on where you are and what type of property you want. If you want to get your first property around where I live in Rickmansworth it will cost you a lot more than if you want to get your first property in Coventry. It depends on the area and also on a number of different factors. There is no 'one size fits all' answer.

How can I find people I can trust to give me the right guidance?

Trust is very important, particularly in development and, I guess, in investment as well. There are people who are looking to make money at other people's expense, actually take money off them and it's naive to assume otherwise. I'd proceed with caution, and make sure that if you're ever, ever going to part with your money and give it to somebody else you do extensive due diligence on that person. Make sure that you hire the very best lawyers, because otherwise you will leave yourself exposed.

21. Jeanette Linfoot

About Jeanette

Jeannette is a high performing corporate CEO-turned-Entrepreneur with a multi-million-pound business portfolio across multiple sectors. She now helps business owners and senior executives take their business and their careers to the next level. Jeannette is an experienced and highly regarded senior executive, property investor and board advisor with over 27 years' global professional experience across the travel, leisure, hospitality and property sectors. She now has a portfolio of businesses, covering property investing, board advisory and business mentoring. Alongside her direct engagements, Jeannette is also an active mentor for the Odgers & Berndtson/UK Hospitality mentoring programme, a judge for Everywoman in Travel and a member of the Travel Advisory Board of the Founders Factory. More recently Jeannette has moved into the world of podcasting as host of her Brave, Bold, Brilliant podcast.

Based	Mumbles, Swansea
Investment location	Mumbles, Manchester, London, Cambridgeshire
Strategies	Luxury serviced accommodation and buy-to-let
Favourite sayings/ affirmations/mottos	Brave, Bold, Brilliant
Three key learnings you would like to share with readers	• Self-belief is the most important thing you can have to be successful in life, business & career. • The formula for success is: Belief + Purpose + Action = Results • You only have one life so make it count. Don't go to your grave with regrets. Better to try than always wonder 'what if?'

Job (if in a job previously)

Prior to her senior engagements with organisations such as TUI, Thomas Cook, First Choice and Saga, where she was CEO of the Travel Division, Jeannette graduated from university with a 1st class BA Hons degree in Economics & Management Studies, before starting her career in UK Government, as an economist.

Jeannette's broader contribution to her industry has been formally recognised. Inducted into the Travel industry Hall of Fame as Businesswoman of the Year she was subsequently acknowledged as 'One of the Most Influential Women in Travel' by the Association of Women Travel Executives.

Why did you leave your job?

To have freedom, choice and flexibility, and to create multiple streams of income and passive income through property.

What do you love about your life now?

I make the rules.

Education, training, learning

Progressive Property Masterclass, VIP, and mentored directly by Rob Moore and Mark Homer.

Favourite books

- Stephen R. Covey, *The 7 Habits of Highly Effective People*
- Sheryl Sandberg, *Lean In*
- Susan Scott, *Fierce Conversations*

Contact details

Website: www.jeannettelinfootassociates.com

Linktree: https://linktr.ee/JLinfoot

Email: jl@jeannettelinfootassociates.com

Jeanette's Answers

How do I choose the right education, training and learning for me?

I think the first thing is to know how best you actually learn, because for some people it's very visual, for some people it's auditory, etc. So, I think, decide what environment and type of learning is good for you first and then after that what I would then do, is take a look at what's out there... See what's happening on social media and do a little bit due diligence before you jump in. If it's free, you can jump in straight away. If it's learning that involves a paid course or something, then I would be looking for recommendations and referrals of the people that have also done that training.

What happens when I start learning and realise there's more I don't know than I do know, or that there's too much to learn?

Well, you've just got to keep going, haven't you? Because there is always more to learn. It's like peeling an onion, you know, and when you're starting in property, you know you don't know anything and then as you actually start to get into it you realise just how much there is still to learn, but that's normal, that's life, that's business. There is nothing new in that, so you just have to keep going and break it down into bite size chunks. You don't have to learn everything straight away, you don't have to do everything straight away but we are all constantly learning until the day we die, we are a work in progress, I believe.

How can I use my thoughts to help me do what I want?

Thoughts lead to feelings and lead to action. So, when you're thinking of something, also think about how it makes you feel and then use that feeling to galvanise action in the moment. I think this is quite good and that could be as something as simple as making a quick phone call or sending an email, but whatever it is just take action – DON'T procrastinate.

How do I know which people to connect with to help me?

Well, I think go for people you naturally gravitate to and this could be on social media OR physically in the room. But you know you have a vibe and you will attract certain people to you and vice versa. So, I would spend time and chat to lots of people, check out lots of people on social media, and then

THE 1ST PLACE.

I would choose my tribe based on what feels right for me and who's the best for me to learn from, who's the best for me to just bounce ideas off, etc.

Is free help real help for me?

Yeah, it can be, but you know... you get what you pay for in this life as well. So, there is some great free information online, from multiple sources. I put lots of content out on my social media, totally for free and there are some amazing golden nuggets in there for people.

BUT... you're gonna expect a certain quality when it's for free, when you actually go into learning in a deeper way. When you pay for something, the quality of what you get will probably be higher, not always, but probably.

How shall I prepare for opportunities?

Have an open mind and a growth mindset. So, always have your radar up, because opportunities are everywhere... but if you have a closed perception of the world, you won't see them and you won't be able to evaluate them in the same way, so you have to have a growth mindset.

Which beginners' property books would you recommend?

Property Investing Secrets by Rob Moore and Mark Homer. Simon Zutshi's *Property Magic* is also good.

Which property strategy should I follow?

The one that's right for you. Row your own boat not somebody else's. So be clear on what you are trying to achieve with property, how that fits in with your other businesses and your personal life and then from there you will know which strategy is right. If you want cash flow, for example, it might be that Service Accommodation or HMOs are better for you. If you want passive income which involves less time involved from you, it might be that a standard buy-to-let property might be the best strategy for you. So, it depends on what you want, really.

How do I get the properties I want?

Well it's a numbers game, so you have got to take the required action. People sometimes make me laugh when they say, 'Oh I'm not getting any deals'. Well, how many viewings have you done this week? How many doors have you knocked on? How many leaflets have you posted? How many letters have you sent? If you want to get deals, you have to put the work in, and you need to be viewing properties and you need to be offering on properties. It's as simple as that.

What kind of money do I need to get my first property?

Well, it depends on what kind of property you're buying. If you're buying a simple two-bed terrace house for £100,000, you know when you're putting a 25% deposit down, you need £25,000 plus the stamp duty at 3% of purchase price and a couple of grand for your legal costs. You might also be doing a £10,000 to £15,000 refurb, so you're probably talking £40,000 in that example. If you're buying a big commercial development or an HMO then the numbers will be a lot bigger.

How can I find people I can trust to give me the right guidance?

I think you have got to surround yourself with the right people. So, I would definitely say you need to put yourself out there and that's either in the online world in terms of social media *or* it's in the physical world. So, networking events, talking to people, finding out whose got the most knowledge or relevant experience and then building a connection. Also, wherever you feel a good rapport with someone and they're your kind of person and you feel that there is trust. They are probably the ones that are going to help you the most.

22. Jez Wood

About Jez

Jez is one of the Founders and Directors of KOVE Properties, a property investment company based in the Northeast. He has the bold vision to improve housing across the UK and has overseen the growth of the company to achieve the milestone of selling 100 deals in under two years and having a staff team of 10. He also won 'Outstanding Achievement' Progressive Property Academy Awards 2021.

Prior to property, he gained a Business Degree (First Class Honours) from Sheffield University. He has background in the charity and business sectors with expertise in project management, business development and marketing. He has managed contracts of up to £6m, with the likes of Vodafone, Deutsche Bank and Deloitte. He also founded his own catering business and spent three years managing coffee shops in London, including winning a 'Best Cafe' award in 2019.

Based	London
Investment location	Northeast
Strategies	BTL/SA/Developments
Favourite sayings/ affirmations/mottos	Life shrinks or expands in proportion to one's courage
Three key learnings you would like to share with readers	• You are enough • Set clear goals and take action • Everything is achievable, you just need to set your mind to believe

Age 39

Job (if in a job previously)

Corporate Project Manager.

Why did you leave your job?

Wanted more autonomy and freedom to make choices for me and my future.

What do you love about your life now?

Having autonomy and the ability to work anywhere.

Education, training, learning

Progressive Property Academy 2020–22.

Favourite books

- Tim Ferriss, *Tools of Titans*
- Stephen R. Covey, *7 Habits of Highly Effective People*
- Andrew Grove, *High Output Management*

Contact details

Website: www.koveproperties.com

Email: jeremy@koveproperties.com

Linktree: https://linktr.ee/koveproperties

Jez's Answers

How do I choose the right education, training and learning for me?

Firstly, what are you looking to learn? What are your goals and time frames? You've got to make sure the training that you're going on is matched to your level of knowledge. For example, there's no point in you going on a three-day advanced property webinar or seminar in commercial development if you're just a beginner.

You've got to make sure it's matched to you and to your level of knowledge and experience. I'd also say that you've got to ensure that your advisor knows what they're talking about –do some due diligence on them and check out their content online. They will normally have quite a lot of content. Make sure they have the experience to back up what they're teaching and make sure that you're comfortable with that.

What happens when I start learning and realise there's more I don't know than I do know, or that there's too much to learn?

That's inevitable whenever you're learning a new area. It opens up a huge can of worms because you see into a field of study that you didn't know really existed. That can feel overwhelming if you're just at the beginning – but that's kind of normal. I wouldn't worry about it. I'd just keep learning at your own pace and not get too hung up on the gaps.

You've got to think about what you've learned to that point already. I do Capoeira which is a Brazilian martial art. I've been doing it six or seven years and I still feel myself as a beginner. I'm comparing myself to the advanced people in the class who have been doing it for fifteen years. I see myself as a beginner and I think I'm really rubbish compared to them, but then an actual beginner comes in the door, and they've never done anything before and I'm teaching them what to do.

I'm still thinking of myself as a beginner with lots to learn, but actually it's easy to forget how much I've learned already, because I'm teaching the beginners. We always focus on the deficit rather than what we've actually learned, or how much we have in the bank in terms of our knowledge and experience.

How can I use my thoughts to help me do what I want?

Mindset is everything. You've got to ensure that you've got the right conditions to have a positive mindset otherwise it's very easy for your brain to trick you into thinking you don't want to get up at 5am and go for that run when it's cold and dark.

We need to put the structures in place to have a positive mindset – eat well, look after yourself, get a good amount of sleep, exercise, be in a positive environment, surround yourself with positive people. If you don't, you'll probably resort to your brain just talking you out of things. That's why having goals is really important. Refer back to those goals on a monthly basis and have good routines and habits in place to ensure that you're making steps towards your goals. If you just left it to your brain, you probably wouldn't succeed.

How do I know which people to connect with to help me?

You need to find people that you connect with, you have things in common with (where there's a personal connection) and you get on with. It's important that it's recognised that you value the other person's time, especially in business – people will always be willing to help each other, but there'll be a cut-off point. That person will have only so much time to give without it becoming too much of a drain on their time.

Is free help real help for me?

It depends on what stage you're at and on your level of experience. There is a lot of excellent information out there on the internet, which will take you quite far in your learning but then it depends on your level of comfort, depends on your risk tolerance, depends on your life experience. It will be able to get you so far, but it really depends on how far and how advanced you're looking to go.

How shall I prepare for opportunities?

With an open mind. Always be open, especially at the beginning. Always be ready to say 'yes' because you just don't know what's going to come of it. Even, for example, if you've had a long day at work and you really don't want to go to a networking event, push yourself, get outside of your comfort zone and say 'yes' to those opportunities that you might have said 'no' to.

Which beginners' property books would you recommend?

- *Multiple Streams of Property Income,* Rob Moore
- *Property Magic*, Simon Zutshi

Which property strategy should I follow?

That has to be a question for yourself. You need to understand what you're looking to get out of property. Do you need short-term cash flow to leave your job or long-term financial security for your pension? That will then dictate what property strategy you go for.

That's the thing to answer – what are you looking to get out of property, what are your goals, where are you in your life. Those answers will determine what property strategy you go for.

How do I get the properties I want?

Relationships, I would say. That's the first and foremost – property is all about relationships, so if you've got the right relationship with agents or sourcing companies or vendors that will probably sway it for you getting that property over other people.

What kind of money do I need to get my first property?

Depends on your strategy and that depends on where you're looking to invest. There isn't a one side splits all answer to that. The answer will be very different if you're looking to buy HMOs in South London or whether you're looking to buy a buy-to-let in Glasgow. It will also depend on what you're looking to get out of property – what your goals are. There isn't a right or wrong answer to that it depends on your circumstance.

How can I find people I can trust to give me the right guidance?

You need to build a relationship with people first before you can trust them. You need to depend on your level of risk tolerance, but it might be worth doing some due diligence as a background check on people if you want to be sure they're trustworthy. Look at what experience they've got, because you don't want to be getting guidance from someone on starting a podcast from someone who's never started a podcast before, for example.

23. John Foster

About John

John Foster is a Chartered Quality Professional with a sharp sense of what it takes to drive results effectively. He has years of high-level experience in quality and has specialised in lean and total quality management. John has worked with many entrepreneurs and businesses to help them maximise their profits and time. He has become known for his ability to provide sound advice while working with property investors, letting agents, manufacturers and a range of other businesses. Valued for his far-reaching expertise as much as for his unbeatable work ethic, he is a highly sought-after consultant and coach. He knows how to manage projects as well as people and is used to performing under pressure, while still delivering the desired results.

John is approachable, captivating when telling stories of his experiences and has a knack for coaching and leading others as he helps them to develop. John strongly believes in the concept of ongoing education, seeking constantly to expand his base of knowledge to better serve his clients.

Based	Solihull
Investment location	South Yorkshire
Strategies	BTL; Creating business management systems for investors
Favourite sayings/ affirmations/mottos	My own motto is 'Life is about adding value to everything that you do.' Others that I use are: • What others think about you is none of your business • Without data you're just another person with an opinion
Three key learnings you would like to share with readers	• Talk to lettings agents and not estate agents about the best areas within your investment area to invest • Get to know your gold mine area well and give the estate agents your hunting brief • • Create your business management systems sooner rather than later

Job (if in a job previously)

Senior Quality Manager in Aerospace.

Why did you leave your job?

I enjoyed it, but the politics at a senior level was unreal. Managers were more about looking out for themselves than working as a team for the good of employees and the company.

What do you love about your life now?

I can pick and choose the work I want to do. I get to meet other investors and help them by creating business management systems to help them become efficient and effective.

Education, training, learning

I did several property training courses, namely:

- Basic property training
- Momentum – advanced property training
- Distressed property
- HMO
- Advance finance
- Commercial conversions
- Accredited Landlord
- Branding & marketing business systems
- Serviced accommodation
- Property tax
- Interior design to increase cashflow

I also worked very closely with three business coaches with many years of experience as professional property investors with multi-million-pound portfolios

Favourite books

- Jeff Olson, *The Slight Edge*
- Napoleon Hill, *Think and Grow Rich*
- Gary Kellar, *The One Thing*

Contact details

Website: www.thebusinesssystemspeople.com

Linktree: https://linktr.ee/TBSP1

Email: john@thebusinesssystemspeople.co.uk

John's Answers

How do I choose the right education, training and learning for me?

Talk to people that have been to the training you'd like to do. Go and talk to the people that run these courses. If they've got some freebies to start with then go to them, get a feel for it and pick up the information that's given out. Then go to as many as possible, go to networking events and ask there as well to narrow it down.

What happens when I start learning and realise there's more I don't know than I do know, or that there's too much to learn?

This can be a bit overwhelming. If, say, you're on a two or three-day course with a lot of things being thrown at you and you're trying to take it all in, it can be difficult. You've got to take notes and things like that. You're usually given a booklet, so go back through that and re-read it. Go through your notes but do it while it's fresh in your mind – if you leave it for weeks, you may forget. You can contact the trainer and providers for things that you're still not sure of and ask questions.

How can I use my thoughts to help me do what I want?

It's having clarity. Mindset is important because it's having clarity of where you want to go and what you're trying to achieve. Think of your end goal and work backwards. So, if in the first instance, all you want to do is get one buy-to-let that's fine. Work backwards from there and ask yourself: Who do I need? How much money do I need? What sort of area do I need? It's important to break things down into small steps so they're manageable and don't overwhelm you.

How do I know which people to connect with to help me?

That can be quite difficult, because at times there are people that have got their own agendas. You're going to have to do your due diligence to help you to decide. Talk to a lot of people, do some networking find out more about them, look at their profiles on social media and follow them to see what they're posting.

Is free help real help for me?

It can be. It depends on what help you're looking for. You know there are genuine people out there who will give you free help, because you're not taking too much of their time. If you're obviously looking at a complete strategy, then you're better off talking to somebody where you have to pay for it. You'll get all the information you need because that's what you're paying for.

How shall I prepare for opportunities?

Opportunities are always out there. It's about keeping eyes and ears open. You need to be open-minded with a lot of these things. See what they are first and whether it's suitable for your needs. It might be an opportunity for a complete portfolio, but you're just getting involved and that's not for you, because it's far too big. But there's an opportunity of passing that on to somebody else and then learning from them, so there's an opportunity there still, but in a different form.

Which beginners' property books would you recommend?

My book called *Right First Time Property Investing the Trilith Way* looks at it from the business side of view. Put in place your systems and your processes first to help you because that makes your property investing easier later on. Rob Moore has a few books that are quite good and Rob Dix too.

Which property strategy should I follow?

I would start with a buy-to-let because that gives you a learning curve that's not going to take up too much. Obviously, it depends on what you've bought. If there's going to be a huge amount of refurbishment, then obviously you've got to allow budgets and things for that, but on the whole it's a cheaper way of getting involved. It's more manageable than HMO or Serviced Accommodation because you're only dealing with one tenant instead of dozens of them.

How do I get the properties I want?

You're never going to get exactly what you want. The important thing is to understand your area and what's going on in it and to put in offers. Unless you put in those offers you're not going to get them. You've got to be persistent and patient. You're going to be seeing lots of viewings and you'll be putting in lots of offers, but you may not necessarily get the property.

What kind of money do I need to get my first property?

You don't actually need your money – it could come from family and friends. Just enough for a deposit or a refurb. There is a strategy where you can buy property for a £1, but that's far more advanced and there's a bit more to it. You can start with very little money and build up from that by having investors, by having a team behind you or JV partners.

How can I find people I can trust to give me the right guidance?

Some people can come from your network, others may recommend people. You can put a post on social media and you'll probably get a whole list of people. Then you've got some names and things to be checking out, whether it's an accountant or a builder or another trade or profession. It's that bit of research you've got to do and do your due diligence, and then once you've decided on the people you're interested in, go and talk to them. See if you can actually work with them and whether they're a good fit for what you want.

24. John Philbin

About John

John rented his first property way back in 1987 with zero advice or education. He now has an impressive multi-million-pound residential and commercial portfolio, a deal sourcing/development company and a lettings agency. John and his wife Melanie also own and operate a chain of award-winning beauty salons. Along the way John has studied person-centred counselling, NLP, hypnosis and reiki healing. MINDSET is of particular interest to him.

Based	Leeds
Investment location	Yorkshire (predominantly)
Strategies	Business; buy-to-let, letting agency, sourcing and, more recently, new builds. Specialities include: single lets, commercial, business, multiple income streams, buy-refurb-refinance, creative property solutions, mindset and title splitting, among others.
Favourite sayings/ affirmations/mottos or key learnings you would like to share with readers	• Anyone can achieve if they want it bad enough. • Do something. There's magic in movement. • Don't listen to the nay-sayers.

Age

55

Job (if in a job previously)

Factory worker.

Why did you leave your job?

I had the chance of redundancy and thought it was time I stopped working.

What do you love about your life now?

Freedom from responsibility.

Education, training, learning?

- Progressive Property Masterclass, and many other courses
- Learning from my own mistakes (boots on the ground learning)
- Now a mentor for Progressive Property
- Person-centred counselling; NLP; Hypnosis

Favourite books

- George S. Clason, *The Richest Man in Babylon*
- Darren Hardy, *The Compound Effect* and *Design Your Best Year Ever*
- Simon Sinek, *Start With Why*
- Prof Steve Peters, *The Chimp Paradox*

- Michael Gerber, *The E-Myth Revisited*
- Anything by Tony Robbins

Contact details

Websites: www.homestorentleeds.co.uk; www.beautymattersleeds.co.uk

Email: john@john-philbin.com

John's Answers

Editorial comment

John has shared this first answer below in response to a question he was asked in a previous interview that will be included in a future book in this series. It is not a question in this book, but these words are shared, because of their direct relevance to many of the questions below and his answers to them:

As long as you've got your WHY document you can always revisit that. It is a working document, so is subject to change, but what you can do is revisit it as a guidance manual.

So, when the questions arise, the idea of change will only be a logistical change and it won't be any grass roots change. The answer will always be in The WHY document – your WHY plan or WHY goals. So, when the next shiny penny pops its head up, revisit your WHY document, and it will tell you whether or not you should follow the new path, stick to the course you have started, or do an amalgamation of the two.

How do I choose the right education, training and learning for me?

Go back to your WHY document. So, if I've chosen nice single let vanilla investment, there's no point in going on a Serviced Accommodation course, just because everyone else in the room is saying what a nice shiny penny it is. After that you're going to need to do your due diligence on the people who are putting the training forward, as there are a lot of sharks out there who just want to get your money.

Also, we have different learning styles, and might prefer to learn from different types of teachers, even preferring either a male or female trainer, for example. There are no right or wrong answers, there's only your answer and how they present. So, do your background checks, then I'd suggest you actually go and meet them face to face to get a feeling for who they are, then it's just a matter of picking one that fits all your criteria.

What happens when I start learning and realise there's more I don't know than I do know, or that there's too much to learn?

I don't think there's ever too much to learn. You can never learn less, can you? So, it's quite good that you can keep learning, as long as you don't lose the focus. If you've picked your specialist subject and you're researching that, and you picked the property type you want to acquire and you've picked the tenant type you want in that property then, actually, there's going to seem not that much to learn, probably. It's only if you start wanting to learn about everything that you lose focus. Stick to your guns, stick to what we discussed from the start, which is think what you want to achieve, think how you're going to achieve it and then research that.

How can I use my thoughts to help me do what I want?

They're the only things that are going to help you do what you want. Your thoughts become your actions and they become your achievements. It's not a matter of how I can use them, it's the only thing you are ever going to be able to use.

How do I know which people to connect with to help me?

You will be ok if you've done you first bit right and you know WHAT you want to achieve, WHERE you're wanting to achieve it, and what kind of PERSON you want to work with.

I know it's a misnomer but create your avatar. Your avatar is going to be the person who you absolutely want to work with. For me, I wouldn't work with people I don't like, and I don't work with people I don't trust. So, if you've done their research and know exactly who you want to work with and have almost built this picture of an avatar, then as soon as you meet them there going to know who they are.

Is free help real help for me?

It can be, but again you've got to have chosen the right person. If you're waiting for a taxi on a dark road at night and someone pulls up and offers you a free ride is it really helpful? Who knows? If it's your mum, it's absolutely helpful! Free help can be helpful through just being in a room of networking individuals where you catch someone having a good day who just feels generous and wants to talk, and you can pick up some helpful information (as long as you are listening and not just waiting for your turn to talk). If you're willing to listen and you know what you're looking for because you've done your research, then yeah it can be.

I'm not saying that you should only go and get free help because I think that can be counterproductive. Ultimately, if you're a person who is never going to pay for anything, then your investments are going to be roughly the same aren't they? You're never going to want to pay for a decent solicitor, you're going to always want the cheapest of something and I think that will reflect in your achievements.

How shall I prepare for opportunities?

Well we've gone through it – you've found out who you want to work with, you've found out exactly why you are doing what you are doing, you've done the research on the area you want to invest in and the tenant type you want to attract, and how that's going to pan out within the business model that you're building. You've got to be in it to come up with a framework to hang this business on, so that moving forward you can actually make it in to a true business where you're not doing all of the work. So, if you do your research and you've got all the answers that you need, that's it – you have to have the courage of your convictions and just go for it.

Which beginners' property books would you recommend?

Some of the property books that I've read have big writing, lots of white space and lots of fluff. I'd recommend any of the ones listed under my favourite books.

Which property strategy should I follow?

For me to answer that, you need to tell me, because only you can know that. Let's suppose we've got a single mum who wants to make a little bit more money. She's time poor and wants to make enough money to spend lots of time with her daughter and go on holidays together. If she says her strategy is going to be rent-to-rent and serviced accommodation that she'll self-manage, well, we can see that that's not congruent, can't we? So, nobody can tell you which one to do, you've got to tell yourself and you do that by doing the research, finding out why, finding out how and then just doing it.

How do I get the properties I want?

Listen, do research and then listen some more. So, instead of talking, which most people like to do, what you need to do is listen and if your head is thinking, 'How can I help this person in front of me?', truly listen to them and come up with a solution to their needs, and that may be a really simple solution. You might say, 'So, I'm willing to give you 6% per year, we do this swap, I sign some paperwork, I've listened to what you wanted and I've done it'.

Same with the vendor, you say, 'How can I help you? How can I...? So, all you're doing is asking basic question all the time: 'How can I help you?' and then you come up with a solution to that. The more solutions you come up with for other people, the more money you will make.

What kind of money do I need to get my first property?

I don't know, because I don't know what your first property is. It might be a large house in London that you're going to convert into HMOs, in which case you need s**tloads of money. It might be a rent-to-rent in Leeds, Manchester or Hartlepool. It's going to be based upon what you need. But the one thing I can absolutely say is, you will need money. All these people who are telling you can do it with absolutely no money, that's absolute rubbish. You have to have some kind of money even if it's only rent-to-rent, so you've got first month's bond and the first month's rent, etc.

How can I find people I can trust to give me the right guidance?

For me, I've looked at who I want to work with, I've checked out their background and they resonate with me. I've then created this avatar of someone that I want to work with, and if these people tick all these boxes, I trust their guidance. I'll repeat what I've said before, it's about how to adapt to change if change is the only constant. Well, if you've got the fundamentals right, the rest is just logistics because all the questions have already been answered.

25. Julie Hogbin

About Julie

Julie Hogbin is a woman on a mission to create and enable Conscious Leadership globally which involves integrating The Conscious Leadership Code©TM into life and business creating true wealth.

Julie is a multi-published author and podcast host (the 'Conscious Leadership' podcast) who lives her values and works with others to discover and harness theirs, changing their lives and business in the process to work in, and with, flow.

Based	Kent
Investment location	Bexleyheath, Kent
Strategies	HMO owned and rent-to-rent (cash flow and equity); Flip and Lease Option in the past, and now looking at the new permitted development opportunities
Favourite sayings/ affirmations/mottos	• Carpe Diem • 'Nothing sits in isolation – connect the dots and create the links', JAH • Do what you love, and you will never work another day in your life
Three key learnings you would like to share with readers	• You are never too old • Self-awareness is key to success • Time is finite and tomorrow never comes

Age 63

Job (if in a job previously)

Loads! ☺ Management Accountant; Financial Accountant; Auditor; Financial Systems Implementor. Partner in a learning and development consultancy.

Why did you leave your job?

It was time; the partnership was imploding and I knew there was something more out there. I didn't know what that was and went exploring.

What do you love about your life now?

Freedom and flexibility to basically do what I want (within reason), with who I want, when I want. Knowing that if I choose to, I would never have to work another day of my life and I am choosing to work rather than having to. I have never looked to build an empire, the way of life suits me fine ☺

Education, training, learning?

- This would fill the book! I have spent well over 100K in the last 10 years and no idea how much before that. I am a lifelong learner and implementer, and it has been my business for over three decades.
- I've studied and worked with: NLP, Coaching, CiPD, CPD, Books, Audio, John Demartini, T. Harv Eker, Tony Robbins, JT Foxx, Wealth Dragons, Progressive, Paul O'Mahoney, Steven Essa, Simon Coulson, Kevin Wright and more in the UK and the States.

- I ran a Property Networking Meet in Kent for two years, a Business Networking Meet in London for a year, and have attended hundreds, if not thousands, of networking meets on all sorts of subjects including two Progressive Property super conferences.

Favourite Books

- James M. Kouzes and Barry Posner, *The Leadership Challenge*
- Richard Koch, *The 80/20 Principle*
- Julie Hogbin, *Stress – The Reality*
- Spencer Johnson, *Who Moved my Cheese?*

Contact details

Website: www.JulieHogbin.com

Linktree: https://linktr.ee/JulieHogbin

Email: Connect@JulieHogbin.com

Julie's Answers

How do I choose the right education, training and learning for me?

Do your research. Work out how you learn best, whether that be reading, listening, in the room or on zoom, online, or a mixture. Work out how far you want to travel if you're going to choose in the room training. Look at the reputation and reviews of a company or an individual that you maybe choosing to learn from. Assess your current knowledge and find something that stretches you. There is so much more to say on this subject but it all comes back to: do the research before you start.

What happens when I start learning and realise there's more I don't know than I do know, or that there's too much to learn?

There's never too much to learn, accept that fact now. You'll never stop learning, because nothing is ever finished, and everything is always evolving. There will always be more to learn. Everything changes from governments to tax rules, regulations to the opportunities for investment.

Work out initially what it is you think you might want to do and then learn about that. Along the way, add in new learning and do not stop learning. You cannot allow the need for learning to stop you from starting, and you need enough learning to start, that is for sure.

How can I use my thoughts to help me do what I want?

Manage your thoughts, listen to your thoughts, and if your thoughts are stopping you – for example, if you've got negative thoughts – think about why that may be. Look at where they've come from – maybe a previous person in your life, your upbringing, your early years. We are imprinted on without knowing it, therefore reflection and analysis of our own thoughts is imperative and then we can change them.

Changing your thoughts to positive and proactive thoughts will give you the agency to move forward and then you can channel those thoughts into the goals and plans you want to achieve. Channel your thoughts to your vision to give yourself the golden thread that links your thoughts to the bright light at the end of the tunnel that you're working towards.

How do I know which people to connect with to help me?

Network: do your research, talk to people get to know them and, again, do your research. I can't emphasise that enough. And work out what it is you're doing and the people that you need around you. Remember, they will change along with your property journey, because as you get bigger you'll be needing to access different set of skills. So, an accountant you might use at the beginning of your property journey is a different person to the one you may need five years down the line. Find people that are in front of you in your journey, and find out who they're utilising. That is a quick tip.

Is free help real help for me?

Sometimes it is and sometimes it's not.

How shall I prepare for opportunities?

Keep your eyes and your ears open to see and hear the opportunities that are around you. And don't be overly excited by opportunities that will completely take you off track, unless those opportunities are on a path, maybe a tributary, to get to where you want to be. You've got to see them, hear them AND acknowledge they are an opportunity, and then work out whether THAT opportunity is one you actually want or need to take.

Which beginners' property books would you recommend?

I don't know because I haven't read any recently. YPN and the Property Investor News magazines are monthly editions – there's very different information in both.

Which property strategy should I follow?

I would say that this depends on:

- Your personality
- Your finance situation
- Where you live
- Your risk profile
- Whether you want tenants or not
- Your ability to deal with people

How do I get the properties I want?

You network; you talk to people; you do your research; you market online and offline; you walk the area that you've decided you want to work in. Whatever property it is you want, it will be in a certain place, whether that's Commercial or Residential. You research the areas, then you walk the areas, then you talk to agents and people that live in the areas. Nothing will beat the groundwork you do and the relationships you build.

What kind of money do I need to get my first property?

Depends entirely on the strategy you're utilising.

How can I find people I can trust to give me the right guidance?

Research. I keep saying that! Research, research, research. Then get yourself out into the environments where you meet people, where you hear people speak, whether that be on social media or physically. Get yourself onto social media platforms where you can hear people's voices. Currently Clubhouse is a really good one, because you can hear people – you can sit in the audience and listen to them on a daily basis if you choose to.

How do you trust them? Do your research, get to know them, listen to them, learn from them and do your research because people can adopt a mask. I wonder how many times I can say, do your research.

26. Kevin Poneskis

About Kevin

Kevin started in property aged 20. His early properties included BTLs and HMOs, all done while climbing to the rank of Regimental Sergeant Major in a Commando Regiment. Kevin served in the Balkans and Afghanistan, but chose to leave in 2011 to embark on a full-time career as a property investor.

Kevin, now known as the Property Soldier, employs multiple strategies including Buy Refurbish Refinance, R2SA, Lease Options, Vendor Finance and Straight Purchase using private and bank finance. Kevin has flipped many properties and is growing his SA portfolio using R2SA, BTL Conversion into SA, Straight Purchase, SA Management and converting B&Bs into Apart Hotels. He also hosts his own podcast – The Serviced Accommodation Property Podcast – and has a YouTube channel: Kevin Poneskis, Property Soldier.

Based	Cambridgeshire
Investment location	UK
Strategies	BTL, HMO, Serviced Accommodation, Hotels
Favourite sayings/ affirmations/mottos	Your Future Needs You
Three key learnings you would like to share with readers	• Have a clear vision of what it is you're trying to achieve and why that is so important to you • Only take advice from people who are successful and therefore qualified to give you advice • Surround yourself with people who are helping and inspiring you

Age 50

Job (if in a job previously)

Army for 24 years

Why did you leave your job?

Freedom

What do you love about your life now?

Freedom

Education, training, learning

Too many to list

Favourite books

- Napoleon Hill, *Think and Grow Rich*
- Robert T. Kiyosaki, *Rich Dad Poor Dad,*
- Dr John Demartini, *The Values Factor*

Contact details

Website: propertysoldier.co.uk

Email: kevin@propertysoldier.co.uk

Kevin's Answers

How do I choose the right education, training and learning for me?

Consume as much pre-content as you can through podcasts and YouTube, then seek out a trainer you see and like, and check if they've got any written material out there. Once you've aligned yourself to a particular type of property investing and a particular trainer or training company, see whether or not you can get on to any free, or low cost, events and try it for size.

What happens when I start learning and realise there's more I don't know than I do know, or that there's too much to learn?

Once you start learning and realise there's a lot you don't know, that's just affirming or reaffirming that you're doing the right thing. You're getting some education because you don't know what you don't know, and that's a scary place to be. For example, in property you might not know what the correct procedure is around

- Insurance
- Compliance
- Planning
- Licensing
- Company structures

You only start to learn that when you get properly educated, and then you realise how much you don't know, which is a good thing. It prompts you to endeavour to continue learning and as long as you do that, and reassure yourself that you're never going to know everything, that's ok. You will definitely know a lot more than the uneducated people out there who are just taking all of the risks, unaware of what risks they're actually taking.

How can I use my thoughts to help me do what I want?

Secrets of a Millionaire Mind by T Harv Eker is a good book to help people with their positive affirmations. You can also Google affirmations and find lots of other resources. We all need daily positive affirmations that are going help create the right mindset. The right type of affirmations are, 'I am XYZ' or, 'I do XYZ' not, 'I must not' or, 'I do not' or, 'I should not'.

Get some knowledge and information around positive affirmations to help you create more positive habits and behaviour.

How do I know which people to connect with to help me?

To start with, getting into a network of like-minded people is always going to help. People who are more entrepreneurial need to surround themselves with like minds. So, get yourself into the right network and the right Facebook groups. Find people who are also interested in what you're interested in, and then it's always good to get referrals and recommendations from those types of people.

Is free help real help for me?

I know somebody who uses the phrase, 'Free advice is worth every penny'. If you've got a friend or family member who's successful in a particular area, and they're willing to give you free training and mentoring, then lucky you. For most of us, we need to seek out somebody who's ultimately willing to help us for a fee.

How shall I prepare for opportunities?

Having the right mindset is going to be very important, because opportunities actually present themselves all the time. When you're not looking for them, or ready to receive them you won't see them. The mind or the 'neck top computer' if you like, is the most important thing. You can go and get as much education as you like – but unless you've got the right mind set to feel worthy of success, to feel worthy of being offered opportunities, then you're not necessarily going to do the things necessary to attract them. You have to know, and genuinely believe, that you deserve money and that you are worthy of success. Opportunities come to people who are ready to spot them and receive them.

Which beginners' property books would you recommend?

It depends on the strategy. My book called *Serviced Accommodation Success* would be a good starting point for somebody wanting to learn about Serviced Accommodation. A good book to understand the mindset of a property investor or business owner would be *Rich Dad Poor Dad.* That helps us understand the difference between good debt and bad debt, assets versus liabilities, and the fact that we should always seek advice from somebody qualified to give us business or investing advice.

Depending on your strategy, go on Amazon or Google books, use the search function and find ones focused on the strategy you're interested in. With any property book, you're never going to get anything really, really advanced. A book isn't going to give you all the pieces of the jigsaw puzzle, but some will give you more than others. Take notice of reviews too and when you're in your networks, ask in that forum if anyone can recommend some really useful books around the strategy.

Which property strategy should I follow?

The one closest to you, which ticks as many boxes depending on your own circumstances. So, if you want the least hassle, it would be single let, where you outsource it to a letting agent as long as you're happy that it's going to be a lower return. Slightly more difficult might be HMO with more moving parts. You can still outsource the management, but there's more decisions to make, but potentially more return. Serviced Accommodation would incur as many decisions as HMO, but as long as you've got the right management give a higher return again.

If you don't want any tenants or guests to rely on for income, then you might do flipping or deal packaging. In my opinion you should invest in an area as close to where you live as you can depending on your own circumstances and preferences.

How do I get the properties I want?

Ultimately it comes down to giving yourself enough opportunity to get the right number of properties that work for your strategy. If you make 100 offers, you're a lot more likely to get the answer yes, than if you only make five offers. Don't be deterred by a no. In fact, a no confirms that you're not offering too much money. If you're getting too many yeses, then you're offering too much money. But this philosophy will only work if you're making lots off offers. You need to properly learn the strategy by getting the best training on it, analyse the suitability of each property depending on your strategy, arrive at your offer price and then make as many offers as you can.

Find properties to offer on via agents (don't just rely on sites like Rightmove and Zoopla to see what agents have because sometimes, especially with the smaller independents, they sometimes only put properties on their own website). Also look at landlords advertising their properties to rent or to sell themselves on online portals, and you could leaflet your goldmine area too.

What kind of money do I need to get my first property?

You don't need your own money and, in some instances, you need very little money – whether it's your own or somebody else's. For instance, you could rent a property and with permission use it as an HMO, or use it as Serviced Accommodation. What you need is the knowledge and education on how to get business in advance of taking on the liability for the property.

If you wanted to buy a property to use as a single let, you'd need to raise a deposit, the conveyancing and stamp duty costs, and often the cost of a refurb. There are people out there who are getting tiny returns on their money in the bank, but the reality is their money is plummeting in value because of inflation. If you use their money and secure that in a property deal – you can give them a much better rate of return than they're getting in the bank. You can offer them a first charge on the property, but it belongs to you. That's how you can buy property with none of your own money. You'll also benefit from the capital appreciation of the property over time, as well as a share of the cashflow while paying interest on the borrowed money.

Another scenario could be that you've got some money, but you need additional money for all the expenditure required. So that could be a straight loan from someone giving them a better rate than they're getting in the bank. In my experience you don't always need to offer security on people's money, people invest with people they know, like and trust, and trust is actually the most important ingredient. If they aren't comfortable with a straight loan, then you can offer security against the property as an option.

How can I find people I can trust to give me the right guidance?

Take advice from your network, depending on the particular strategy that you want to learn more about. Get recommendations, seek them out on social media, find out if they've got a podcast, see if they've got a book and then attend a free event or something like that and make a decision at that event whether to go forward.

27. Kim Hendle

About Kim

Kim left her corporate job at 57. She took her 21-year-old nephew to a MSOPI event and that started their property education. They started with just the knowledge and experience of Kim buying her own home. Flips were their chosen strategy, and their first purchase was a three-bed, mid-terraced property, which they turned into an eight-bed all en-suite HMO! Now she takes large old, tired buildings back to brick and turns them into high-end, all en-suite HMOs for professionals.

Examples of first 3 properties:

Property 1 = Purchase Price £215k, Refurb £80k, Revalued @ £500k, Income £50k p.a.

Property 2 = Purchase Price £287k, Refurb £100k, Revalued @ £500k, Income £55k p.a.

Property 3 = Purchase Price £320k, Refurb £150k, Revalued @ £760k, Income £81k p.a.

Based	Kettering
Investment location	Northamptonshire
Strategies	HMO, BTL
Favourite sayings/ affirmations/mottos	• JFDI (just f***ing do it!) • Keep doing the same thing and nothing changes
A key learning you would like to share with readers	• You're never too old or too young to start something different

Age 62

Job (if in a job previously)

Business Analyst/Project Manager.

Why did you leave your job?

Voluntary redundancy.

What do you love about your life now?

I love learning something new every day AND not having to put up with others' bureaucracy.

Education, training, learning

Prince 2, ISEB, and a number of property related courses and mentorship.

Favourite books

Haven't got time to read.

Contact details

Email: team.kineticproperty@yahoo.com

Kim's Answers

How do I choose the right education, training and learning for me?

You need to be able to go out and talk to people and get a feel for the different types of training. You can spend thousands of pounds on training and education, but if it doesn't resonate with you, if it doesn't grab your attention or feel right for you, you're unlikely to do something with what you've learned, and then it's wasted money.

What happens when I start learning and realise there's more I don't know than I do know, or that there's too much to learn?

There's never too much to learn. Everyday should be a learning day. We all learn something new every day, which is great. It's one of the reasons I love doing this – because I haven't stopped learning. This is a business, it's a job and you have to learn the skills, the techniques, and the knowledge that goes with it. You shouldn't expect this to be simple or easy. You may get told it is, but it's a whole new skillset and there should be loads to learn – don't be frightened of it.

How can I use my thoughts to help me do what I want?

Well, it kind of depends on how random your thoughts are. Sometimes thoughts alone can stop you doing what you need to do, because you talk yourself out of things. Or, you can think more positively and rationally, and just get on with it. Find reasons to do something, rather than that find reasons not to do it.

How do I know which people to connect with to help me?

Connect with as many people as you can, and then find out who are the people are that can help you. You can't go out and just target somebody, because you don't know whether they're going to help you or if you're going to get on with them. They may not talk your language or understand the strategy you may be working on. Talk to everybody and build relationships with people. Don't just target a person for what you think they can do for you. How do you know if someone can, or will, help you unless you've built a relationship with them?

Is free help real help for me?

Yes of course it is. *If* it's the right kind of help you need.

How shall I prepare for opportunities?

Find an opportunity and then prepare. Become mentally prepared for an opportunity to arise.

Which beginners' property books would you recommend?

I can't recommend any, as I'm not a book reader. I'm too busy 'doing' to make time to read.

Which property strategy should I follow?

When you understand what your goals are, choosing a strategy becomes a lot easier. Although we started off looking at doing flips because we didn't want to have tenants, we ended up developing HMOs. We realised we needed a regular income coming in to get my nephew out of his day job. So, we changed strategies, so we could develop a regular income, but that wasn't what we started doing. We reviewed our goals and adjusted our strategy accordingly.

THE 1ST PLACE.

How do I get the properties I want?

Go out and look for them.

What kind of money do I need to get my first property?

Depends on what getting your first property means. Does it mean buying and owning it yourself, or managing it? If you're looking at managing, then there's rent-to-rent and lots of other strategies out there where you don't need to have money. If you want to buy your own property, then you're going to need at least 25% deposit. You'll also need money for solicitors' fees and so on, whether you use your own money or other people's money.

How can I find people I can trust to give me the right guidance?

Build relationships. You'll get to know who you can work well with, who you trust and who they know. So, just go out there and start talking to people. Don't necessarily make it about property – build a relationship with people first.

28. Lorraine Harris

About Lorraine

Lorraine has been a landlord since 2008, and loves working with people to create win-wins. She started with single lets but soon became an HMO specialist and her team now runs the largest HMO agency in Leicester for working professionals: Best City Rooms.

Originally from Leicester herself, Lorraine lived in France for 25 years and owned a motorcycle business there. She's been back home in her native city since 2018 and loves it. 'Leicester has become such an amazing multi-cultural place, I love the interaction of different cultures and traditions, and having travelled extensively myself, really enjoy welcoming newcomers to our city and helping them find a home.'

Based	Leicester, Malta, and Alsace, France
Investment location	Leicester
Strategies	HMO acquisition, Guaranteed rent, single-let, refurbs, developments
Favourite sayings/ affirmations/mottos	• It's all alright • I lead and inspire others with empathy and kindness, demonstrating self-belief and joy
Three key learnings you would like to share with readers	• Mindset is key • Learn from professionals • • Best business is ethical and win-win

Job (if in a job previously)

I've always worked for myself.

What do you love about your life now?

Freedom, choice, control.

Education, training, learning?

- Honours Degree in Applied languages
- Tigrent property training/mentorship
- Tycoon property training/mentorship
- Multiple courses for different property strategies including HMOs, Guaranteed Rent, Social Housing, Creative Finance, Developments, Systems and Outsourcing

Favourite books

- Eckhart Tolle, *The Power of Now*
- Eckhart Tolle, *A New Earth*
- John Kehoe, *Mind Power into the 21st Century*
- Gary Keller, *The One Thing*
- Brian P. Moran, *The 12 Week Year*

THE 1ST PLACE.

Contact details

Website: www.bestcityrooms.co.uk

Email: lorraine@bestcityrooms.co.uk

Lorraine's Answers

How do I choose the right education, training and learning for me?

Three things:

- Work out what you want, and why you want it.
- Speak to people who are already where you want to be and get recommendations.
- Then do your own due diligence.

What happens when I start learning and realise there's more I don't know than I do know, or that there's too much to learn?

There will always be more, that's life and it's wonderful. You just need to learn the bit that you need in order to take your first steps, then do it progressively, and in bite-size chunks.

How can I use my thoughts to help me do what I want?

You create your reality through your thoughts, so become aware of them first of all, as they have got you where you are now. The more you focus your attention on the reality you wish to create, the easier it will become to achieve your goals ... where attention goes, energy flows.

How do I know which people to connect with to help me?

You won't know until you start. It's a good idea to offer your help at the outset, and then good people will come naturally to you.

Is free help real help for me?

Yes, it can be; you don't have to pay for help. Help is a two-way thing as well. You can help people in certain ways and they help you back. So free help can be very valid, yes.

How shall I prepare for opportunities?

Enjoy your journey, be optimistic, satisfied and receptive to them.

Which beginners' property books would you recommend?

Simon Zutshi *Property Magic* is a good beginners' guide.

Which property strategy should I follow?

That all depends on what you want and why you want it. It will be different for everybody. You might be looking for cash flow to replace your day job, or you might want capital appreciation to help finance your children's studies in 10 years' time. Why you want to invest in property and what you want from it are the questions you first need to answer, then you can work out which strategy is best suited and the skills you need to learn.

How do I get the properties I want?

You set your criteria, research what's available, and create a marketing funnel for finding them.

What kind of money do I need to get my first property?

The easiest way is to have the money for a deposit and works, but there are creative ways of financing acquisitions without cash too.

How can I find people I can trust to give me the right guidance?

By getting out there and mixing with people; going to local property meets; attending online webinars ... you need to build your network and trust.

29. Michelle Walker Smith

About Michelle

I have always been a people person and believe that everyone can take control of their happiness. After completing my business degree at 24, I secured a position within Housing and Property Management – and remained in this industry for over 25 years. Having owned a portfolio for a number of years with my husband, in 2015 I set up the award-winning Aqua Lettings Ltd, which has an outstanding reputation in the North East. I will always give back wherever possible and enjoy being a successful Property Mentor, helping others who wish to get started in the property industry. I help to guide and advise wherever I can.

Peter and I now own 17 properties. We also have 14 properties that we run through Lease Options. I am an award-winning author and business owner, I personally won the Fabulous Friend Award Issued by NE Youth International Women's Day Awards March 2021, reached the National Business Women's Awards in the Best New Business category and Business Woman of the Year Micro (Less than £1 Million turnover) and Northern England Business Woman of the Year. I was nominated for Female Entrepreneur of the Year 2022, and was a finalist for Author of the Year 2022. In Association with my company, Aqua Lettings, I was awarded Winner of Property Management Services 2021/2022 and received the Silver Employment Recognition Award Issued by Armed Forces Covenant, May 2021.

Based	Morpeth, Northumberland
Investment location	South Northumberland / Newcastle upon Tyne
Strategies	Single Buy-to-lets / HMO / SA / Lease Options / Starting Businesses from scratch
Favourite sayings/ affirmations/mottos	'If you see someone without a smile, give them one of yours', and 'Be the best version of you that you can be'.
Three key learnings you would like to share with readers	• Don't expect to be perfect straight away • It isn't a get rich quick system • Mindset is key

Age 50

Job (if in a job previously)

Housing and Property Management.

Why did you leave your job?

To set up Aqua Lettings Ltd.

What do you love about your life now?

The freedom it gives me. The fact I help change peoples' lives – be it tenants, landlords or people starting on their property journey.

Education, training, learning?

- Business Degree 2:2 (hons)

- Progressive Property – Entrepreneurs Business Academy/Business Marketing Mastermind/Inner Circle Mastermind – Elite
- Mindset Mastery (3-month PD course)
- Co-Author of the book *Stronger Than Ever: Empowering Stories from 16 Courageous Female Entrepreneurs* by Queens in Business
- Host of the networking group, Property Investors North East (PINE) where my love of connecting people shines through

Favourite books

- Eckhart Tolle, *Breaking the Habit of Negative Thinking and Self-talk*
- Steve Peters, *The Chimp Paradox*
- Daniel Priestly, *Key Person of Influence*
- Rob Moore, *Life Leverage*

Contact details

Websites: www.michellewsmith.co.uk; www.aqualettings.co.uk

Email: michelle@aqualettings.co.uk

DEDICATION

My contribution is dedicated to Peter, who started us on this journey, and my three beautiful reasons WHY: Nathan, Jessica and Patrick. You all are my world, without you three, there would be no reason.

Michelle's Answers

How do I choose the right education, training and learning for me?

I think research, reviews, talking to people who've been through which ever courses you decide you want to do. You have to think of your strategy, whether it's deal sourcing, buy-to-lets or commercial. You have to choose your strategy first, then look at which organisations do the courses. Then look at reviews, talk to people who have been on the courses and you'll find them on various Facebook groups. Ask them what they took from the courses, what wasn't so good from the courses and you know you might have to kiss a few frogs before you find your prince.

What happens when I start learning and realise there's more I don't know than I do know, or that there's too much to learn?

Don't panic about it, you can only take things one step at a time so you learn what you can until you feel comfortable with that and then you move on to the next stage. Don't get overwhelmed by it all, make notes. Everybody starts their property journey somewhere, so you just have to be mindful that you're not going to learn it all straight away. Just take things at your own pace because everybody's property journey is different.

How can I use my thoughts to help me do what I want?

You can choose your thoughts, you're in control of your thoughts and I know from experience that positivity breeds positivity just like negativity breeds negativity. So, if you're constantly thinking of the positives, you'll attract more positivity, and you will attract success. So, I think you just have to remain positive with your thoughts. You won't all the time – everyone is human – but you have to try even if it's a little mantra in the morning. I physically sometimes have to push negative thoughts out of my head and it works.

How do I know which people to connect with to help me?

If you have an instant rapport with them, talk to them. Either meet them or have a zoom with them, if they're not from the area. I think you just know if the conversation flows and you feel comfortable and at ease with them. General rule of thumb is that, with people I've met in property, everybody wants to help each other and will share their knowledge. Be mindful, go with your gut and don't be surprised if you do come across a few bad apples but just move on because it's their problem, not yours.

Is free help real help for me?

Yes, I think it can be. From my perspective, because I'm going to promote my own personal brand and would like to get into mentoring, I would rather help somebody on their way for free to start with, because I would like to hope that somewhere along the line it will come back. I suppose the knack is to realise how genuine people are and if they expect something back then their help is not for free.

How shall I prepare for opportunities?

If you have your ultimate goal in mind and you know which strategy you want to take or want to achieve, and you put yourself in the way of opportunities, as in networking and telling people what you're doing, you will find that opportunities come to you. If you have to search for them too much you might put a block on yourself. So, work on your mindset, work on talking, getting out there, letting people know what you're doing and opportunities will come to you. Have a plan, don't be scared. Believe in the process.

Which beginners' property books would you recommend?

Multiple Streams of Property Income by Rob Moore and Mark Homer (version 3 by Rob Moore and Kevin McDonnell), *Life Leverage* by Rob Moore, and *Rich Dad Poor Dad* by Robert Kiyosaki.

Which property strategy should I follow?

Personally, I wouldn't go too big too quickly. If you haven't done property at all, I would stick with buy-to-lets to start with and get a couple of them under your belt so that you build your knowledge and experience.

If you've no experience with the commercial side, for example, be careful that you don't jump in too quickly with something that's a massive risk. I know people do it and succeed at it, but personally, I think the vanilla buy-to-lets are a brilliant foundation to start and once you've got to grips with them you can get building your passive income and leave them to run themselves. Then, if you choose, go and get your education for something bigger, whether it's HMOs or Service Accommodation or whatever strategy you might want to do

How do I get the properties I want?

At the moment I think it's very difficult, and that there are many folks looking for the same below market value properties. We found that it is hard work and you've got to push through and keep going – the deals are out there. Keep shouting about what you do, you never know who might be watching. My business isn't deal sourcing, but I've got people who come to me with the properties to sell or whatever, so I pass them on to our investors. So, again, if you're in the right mindset, the correct properties will come to you.

We had properties come to us because of the good working relationship we had with our contractor. He brought them to us on behalf of a tired landlord. Building up trust with a trustworthy deal sourcer who has a good track record takes time. It's all about the relationships. I'm very conscious that the opportunities and the properties will come to you once you have built up your track record – be it with relationships with the sourcers, estate agents and contractors. I'm a firm believer if it's meant to be it will be.

What kind of money do I need to get my first property?

Other people's money. It would be lovely to have an infinite amount of money that you could call upon, but unfortunately in the real world it doesn't work like that. You could try and get an investor to do some sort of joint venture with you. Or you could ask your family if anyone has got any savings in the bank that may not be getting the best interest rates. Tell them what return you can give them if you buy a property for them. You'd need your figures to know how much you'd need, such as for the deposit and if any refurbishment is required.

How can I find people I can trust to give me the right guidance?

You have to build up the relationships. You've got to put in what you wish to get out. You've got to trust your instincts or you will get your fingers burned. I think communication is key – if you're not happy, you've got to communicate that. Build the trust through time, but again it is communication and, with me, it's always going back to the gut feeling. If you do trust somebody instinctively, I think you know whether they're a good egg or not and you get that rapport with them. I think it's the same with education, you've got to build up that trust to start with and just be aware to be protected if things were to go pear-shaped.

30. Motiul Islam

About Motiul

Motiul's property journey begun at the age of 19 when he was at university. While his peers were in lectures, he was stepping out of the lecture theatre to negotiate deals. He learned some crucial lessons early on when he was 'gazumped' in each of his first three property deals.

However, he didn't let this stop him and by the age of 23, he had bought his first property investment. He continued to buy subsequent properties one after another, employing no money down strategies before they were even taught and adding value to properties through a combination of extending, developing and carrying out title splits.

In addition to his property businesses and interests, Motiul is the co-host of monthly property networking events at PPN Stratford, has his own YouTube channel and is a Director of World Game Changers CIC.

Portfolio Value: £3.5m+Monthly income: £20k+

Based	London
Investment location	National
Strategies	Lease Options, Vendor Finance, Short leases, Title splits, Commercial conversions, HMOs
Favourite sayings/ affirmations/mottos	• If you think you can or you think you can't. You're right. (Henry Ford)
Three key learnings you would like to share with readers	• Value your health and time • Invest in your knowledge and mindset • Leverage everything

Age 43

Job (if in a job previously)

IT

Why did you leave your job?

Property was more lucrative.

What do you love about your life now?

Spending time with family and having choice.

Education, training, learning

- Progressive VIP/Academy
- Deal Packaging
- Commercial Conversions
- Expert Speaker Revolution & Academy

- Public Speakers University
- Facebook & Funnels Academy
- Guerrilla Marketing Bootcamp

Favourite books

- Robert Kiyosaki, *Rich Dad Poor Dad*
- Napoleon Hill, *Think and Grow Rich*
- Dale Carnegie, *How to Make Friends and Influence People*

Contact details

Website: motiul.co.uk

Linktree: https://linktr.ee/motiul

Email: motiul@icloud.com

Motiul's Answers

How do I choose the right education, training and learning for me?

Personally, I find I retain more information by doing something. I prefer being around people, being positive and having fun and enjoying it. I seem to retain information better when I'm enjoying something.

What happens when I start learning and realise there's more I don't know than I do know, or that there's too much to learn?

Every day is a school day. You can never learn everything, but I would say at least try and specialise in something.

How can I use my thoughts to help me do what I want?

Everything starts with a thought. So, if you're thinking about where you want to get to and it's constantly on your mind in the background, try and work out a way to achieve it.

How do I know which people to connect with to help me?

Regular networking will help. Find people that resonate with you – people that are doing the things you want to do and are achieving the results you're hoping for. The more you network the more you're going to build your power team. That's where you're going to find people who will connect you to the people you want to be connected to.

Is free help real help for me?

Sometimes, but not always. There is only a limited amount of free help.

How shall I prepare for opportunities?

Put yourself in the position where you can take advantage of opportunities.

Which beginners' property books would you recommend?

Robert T Kiyosaki, *Rich Dad Poor Dad*

THE 1ST PLACE.

Kevin McDonnell, *No Money Down*

Napa Bafikele, *The Rent to Rent Blueprint*

Which property strategy should I follow?

This is different for every individual. That's why there are so many strategies that people are doing. Choose the one that you'll be able to do best, not the one that makes the most money. The one that you can do best, is the one that'll make you the most money.

How do I get the properties I want?

Depending on the strategy, it's pretty much following the routes that are taught. So, for no money down lease options – find out how lease options are done, where to find them, who to approach and then how to do them. For straightforward buy-to-lets or BRRs – find out how to source them, what to do with them and then how to refinance and move on to the next one.

What kind of money do I need to get my first property?

Money (as in your own money) isn't necessarily needed. Money is always needed to do a property transaction, but if you're willing to put in your time and effort, or you have a skillset to put towards it, money is not always necessary.

How can I find people I can trust to give me the right guidance?

You need to speak to a lot of people and find out what they've found useful. The one-day events where they sell you lots of courses are probably not the best places. Maybe attend them a few times, but do your research. Research the trainers, the training companies, see what their backgrounds are, what their achievements are, what their reviews are like and only after that would I then choose a company to go with.

31. Muzzie Nduna

About Muzzie

I was born in Zimbabwe and moved to the UK at 17 in 2004.

I studied Manufacturing Engineering and worked in the automotive industry in the West Midlands area of the UK becoming a Production Manager in charge of over 70 employees at the age of 27. I got into property in 2018 through training courses and subsequently acquired HMOs and serviced accommodation units on a rent-to-rent and buy-to-let basis in the West Midlands, and I currently manage a portfolio of over 30 properties. I also have a YouTube channel.

Based	Nuneaton
Investment location	West Midlands
Strategies	Rent to Serviced Accommodation
Favourite sayings/ affirmations/mottos	If you want to go fast, go alone. If you want to go far, go together.
Three key learnings you would like to share with readers	• Find your WHY and hold on to it • Educate yourself • TAKE ACTION

Age 35

Job (if in a job previously)

Business Improvement manager

Why did you leave your job?

I had achieved all I wanted in the corporate world and the next stage of my life was found in business.

What do you love about your life now?

Watching my wife put her heart and soul into her passion because our business took her out of her job.

Education, training, learning

- Multiple Streams of Property Income
- No Money Down Strategies
- Property Investment for Beginners course

Favourite books

- Simon Sinek, *Start with Why*
- Robert T. Kiyosaki, *Rich Dad Poor Dad*
- Viktor Frankl, *Man's Search for Meaning*

THE 1ST PLACE.

Contact details

Linktree: www.dibiz.com/muzzie-nduna

Email: info@imanipi.co.uk

Muzzie's Answers

How do I choose the right education, training and learning for me?

It comes down to what you resonate with. Understand what's being offered and understand what you like and how you like to be taught, and then mix it with what you're looking to learn.

What happens when I start learning and realise there's more I don't know than I do know, or that there's too much to learn?

Then that's a brilliant position to be in, because you know exactly where you are. Now you can start making a plan of where you want to be.

How can I use my thoughts to help me do what I want?

Every single thing that you do starts from thought, so utilise the skill set that you have had since you were born and take action.

How do I know which people to connect with to help me?

It starts from knowing yourself and where you want to be. Once you get to know that, the more people you start meeting, the more you'll realise which ones are going your direction and which ones are not.

Is free help real help for me?

Help that comes towards you will be great help. As long as you understand where you want to be, you will understand. Whether it's free or not doesn't necessarily matter. You will know whether this is good for you or not.

How shall I prepare for opportunities?

Opportunities come to you when you work on yourself, so the best thing to do is work on your personal development.

Which beginners' property books would you recommend?

Kevin McDonnell's book, *No Money Down Property Investing*, and *Rich Dad Poor Dad* by Robert Kiyosaki.

Which property strategy should I follow?

One that resonates with your personality.

How do I get the properties I want?

You get the properties that you want based on the knowledge that you've accumulated and that marries up again with your personality.

What kind of money do I need to get my first property?

That depends on the strategy you're deciding to go for – the knowledge you've created might actually make you realise that you don't need any money to start with.

How can I find people I can trust to give me the right guidance?

A bit like success, the more you work on yourself, the more you attract the people you will need.

32. Natalie Bailey

About Natalie

Natalie Is a Confidence Coach, Property Developer, public speaker and podcast host (Confidence Mastery: Unlock Your Life) who helps entrepreneurs to shift their mindset to one of abundance and confidence. With big projects on the horizon to match the

30-unit, health development currently under construction, she is on a mission with her business partner, Paula Bailey, to help create community to provide unity and belonging.

Natalie also enjoys teaching the triangle of life: Health, Wealth and Happiness, to help others create the lives they truly deserve. From online coaching to retreats in Barbados, she believes there is a way for anyone to work and make an impact on their world.

Based	Worldwide
Investment location	East Anglia
Strategies	Commercial Conversions
Favourite sayings/ affirmations/mottos	Consistency = Success
Three key learnings you would like to share with readers	• Asking for help makes you stronger. • Say Yes and figure it out as you go – you learn by doing. • • Looking after your health is the best way to get mental clarity for your business. Healthy body, healthy mind.

Age 31

Job (if in a job previously)

Previously a PT and Boxing Gym owner.

Why did you leave your job?

I was unfulfilled, my Nan passed away and I wanted to spend more time creating a legacy with my Mum.

What do you love about your life now?

The freedom it represents, the opportunity to network with like-minded people, and the ability to help people not only with creating new homes but also to make more money and increase their confidence.

Education, training, learning?

I've completed many property training courses with Progressive Property and Assets for Life. I've also done Public Speaker training, coaching courses and more.

Favourite books

- Ichiro Kishimi and Fumitake Koga, *The Courage to be Disliked*
- Gay Hendricks, *The Big Leap*

- George S. Clason, *The Richest Man in Babylon*

Contact details

Websites: www.baileyenterprises.org; www.nataliearabella.com

Natalie's Answers

How do I choose the right education, training and learning for me?

Look at the different options available. You could,

- Go to free events (leave your credit card at home)
- Spend some time with those people
- Speak to people that have done training with those trainers

Then make an informed decision. Now, you can get your wallet out – but there's no need to run to the back of the room for the 'deal', as there'll always be another deal to be had. Make sure it's what you really want and need, and if that particular training will help you get there. If the answer is YES – then do it. If the answer is NO – don't do it.

What happens when I start learning and realise there's more I don't know than I do know, or that there's too much to learn?

There's too much to learn in the world, anyway! Your brain can't handle all the information in the world so don't worry about that. As you grow, you will have team members and people that can help you for the bits that you don't understand. You don't need to know everything to get ahead, you need the right network and help.

You will need to know the basics: what are the main things? You can find, learn from and work with specialists for whatever you don't know. As an example, for my business, we've got a 30-unit development. We've got contractors, a site manager and bricklayers, etc., plus many other trades and professionals that work with and for us. Bricklayers know how to build the walls, BUT they don't necessarily know how to put the roof on. That's what the roofers do! You have the different moving parts; you create a team. You can't know it all. You don't need to know it all and you especially don't need to know it ALL before you get started.

How can I use my thoughts to help me do what I want?

Personally, I think there are two kinds of self-talk: negative self-talk and positive self-talk.

A lot of us beat ourselves up for not quite getting something right or for something we've said or done. People just beat themselves up unnecessarily. So, when you notice that you are doing these things and you're speaking to yourself like that, think to yourself, 'Would I speak to my child like that? or a friend? or a sibling? or my parents?' The answer probably is 'no'. So, why would you speak to yourself like that? So, if you treat yourself as if you were your own child, you'll be a lot kinder to yourself, you'll be a lot more positive and that will help you to do more.

How do I know which people to connect with to help me?

You don't. You may never know! But you can learn, and this comes with experience –through talking to people and being open to conversations, learning about them as a person, as a business owner, and trusting your gut. Your gut will tell you a lot. If something doesn't feel right about a person, you're probably right and if it does you are probably right, too. Obviously, our radars can be off sometimes, but it comes through conversation and not being afraid to keep having conversations where you will learn. Do a bit of digging on people, check out their social media, how they speak with other people and treat them. I always say it's ok to do a bit of online stalking, just don't do it in person!

Is free help real help for me?

Free will only get you so far. It's definitely possible to do things without paying but it isn't always the best use of your time. I see a lot of people saying you can get all of this information online. Yes, you can, but when something is in a succinct format that's easy for you to follow all in one place you are going to get the answers and the results a lot quicker.

So, it depends on how fast and how far you want to go.

How shall I prepare for opportunities?

Being open to saying 'yes'. Honestly, this frustrates the hell out of me because people just don't say yes enough. They say "I want this, I want that, I want this" and then they're presented with an opportunity, and they do nothing with it. Wasn't it Richard Branson who said "Say YES and figure it out later?", so just be open to receive and say YES and figure out later on.

Which beginners' property books would you recommend?

Beginners Guide to Property Investing by Rob Moore, and Robert T. Kiyosaki's *Rich Dad, Poor Dad* – that one's a staple.

Which property strategy should I follow?

The one that's going to get you the life that you want.

It's important to bear in mind, just because something works for someone else, it doesn't mean it's going to work for you. You have to think about your life and the lifestyle that you want. So, consider, what do you want to spend your days doing? HMOs can be pretty hands on if you're managing them yourself. Do you want to be talking to tenants (all the time)?

Serviced Accommodation? You're talking to guests all the time. Commercial Conversion – you're talking to Agents; you're talking to landowners; you're talking to contractors. It depends who you want to spend your time talking to and what you want to be doing with your day. That will give you the answer.

Thinking about this is the only way to figure out which strategies are going to work best for your life. It will depend on what you know you might want – even if it's millions and millions and millions of pounds. You know you can achieve that over whatever period of time you want, depending on what strategy you choose, but equally, it comes down to what you want to spend your day doing. Knowing that is going to be the only thing that is going to help you achieve your goals because if you're doing something you don't enjoy you won't do it.

How do I get the properties I want?

Remove the emotion from the property, because it's just a building. There will be another deal to be had. If there's a deal that doesn't work, don't pay over the odds for it, you have to see it as a business transaction. If the numbers don't work, let it go and move on, you will find something else. It's a numbers game – just take away all emotion and then you'll get the deals that work as opposed to a particular property, because if you invest emotionally into a property, you'll end up paying too much for it and then it won't stack.

What kind of money do I need to get my first property?

Depends on what your first property is. The first property I ever bought was a 20,000 sq ft former care home and I didn't use any of my money in the beginning. I don't want to say that you don't need any of your own money, because you do – you need to have resources available, even if just for travel and looking around. So, there isn't a magic number. It depends on the strategy and the deal.

How can I find people I can trust to give me the right guidance?

How you find the people is by networking, by talking to people in online communities,

By going to property specific events, and by finding the people that are doing what you want to do. Put yourselves in front of those people and make friends.

It sounds a bit odd, but if there is someone that you really want to get to know, then social media has made things so much easier to get in front of people that 20 years ago wouldn't have been possible. Start commenting, talking to them, posting in their groups. You build up a relationship with all sorts of people that way, but you need to get out and about in person, too. You can't beat in person meetings. Get to networking events, talk to people – just don't be afraid to talk to people and don't be afraid to tell them you're new because we were all new once.

33. Natasha Collins

About Natasha

I'm Natasha Collins, Founder and CEO of NC Real Estate.

I'm a chartered surveyor who specialises in asset management and property investment strategy, and I've been in the property industry since 2009. I am a property investor and invest in both residential and commercial property from London to the South West of the UK to the USA. Additionally, I host the Honest Property Investor podcast and have my own YouTube channel.

My role, is putting together portfolio strategies. The most important values I hold are trust and honesty. I don't talk 'financial freedom' or '6-figure salaries'. I'm all about smart tactics, building your investments wisely, caring for your tenants and having a lot of fun along the way. I understand that any property you purchase has to suit your goals, lifestyle and risk appetite, therefore each strategy I build is individual to the investor.

Based	Currently: Austin, Texas
Investment location	South of England and the USA
Strategies	Commercial, Mixed Use, Residential, SA
Favourite sayings/ affirmations/mottos	As long as no one has died you get to go again.
Three key learnings you would like to share with readers	• No two properties are the same therefore you can't expect to do exactly the same as someone else. • Focus on your goals and your whys, no one else's. • • Anyone who tells you property is 'passive' is wrong. It takes a lot to buy and hold property, you always need to be making smart decisions, it takes work to create 'passive' income.

Age 32

Job (if in a job previously)

I worked as a lettings agent whilst completing my undergraduate degree before becoming CEO of NC Real Estate.

Why did you leave your job?

I finished my degree.

What do you love about your life now?

I can work from anywhere in the world and at the hours I want.

Education, training, learning?

- BSc Hons – Geography and Computing (Joint Honours)
- MSc – Surveying
- MRICS – Chartered Surveyor

- FHEA – Fellow of the Higher Education Academy
- Asset Manager 2010–present
- Prior to that worked as a lettings agent whilst completing my undergraduate degree.

Books read this year

- James Clear, *Atomic Habits: An Easy and Proven Way to Build Good Habits and Break Bad Ones*
- Dan Harris, *10% Happier*
- Brianna West, *The Mountain is You*

Contact details

Website: ncrealestate.co.uk

Linktree: https://linktr.ee/natashaccollins

Email: natasha@ncrealestate.co.uk

Natasha's Answers

How do I choose the right education, training and learning for me?

You choose the one that looks the most interesting to you because then you will actually do it.

What happens when I start learning and realise there's more I don't know than I do know, or that there's too much to learn?

There is always too much to learn, because the property industry changes. Don't stop doing research about what's going on in the industry and learning new things because legislation changes on a monthly basis. The mortgage lending market changes on a monthly basis. You have to be committed to be a lifelong learner in property and if you look at it like that, starting to pick up knowledge makes it far easier to absorb – you never stop learning in this industry ever. So, the fact that you want to know it all is great but trust me, I don't think anybody knows it all.

How can I use my thoughts to help me do what I want?

That's really good question actually and I have to spend a lot of time on mindset myself. I always think anything is possible in property provided you haven't killed someone! With that being said, rather than thinking I can't do this, change the question to, 'How can I do this?' and keep asking people until you get an answer that might help you move that tiny step forward. You are always going to get people in this industry who say, 'No, it's not a good deal, you can't get finance on that'. Your job is as a property investor is, if you can see a glimmer of that deal working out, you need to make sure you ask every single person until you get the answer that you want to move forward.

How do I know which people to connect with to help me?

Just keep asking questions, you have no idea who you're going to come across in the industry. Some people you get a gut feeling about that they are just not the best and other people you feel they know what they're doing.

There is also always going to be an element in the industry of getting burned. The property industry can be tough, really tough, so my thought process is just reach out and ask people questions when you need to ask questions.

You don't always have to be networking either because sometimes you've actually got to be doing not networking. Networking can hold you back as well. So, when you've got questions, start asking, and if someone comes to you and asks you a question then the decent thing to do is answer that question as well. Knowledge sharing is huge, and you might get an answer that you don't agree with, fine, but you've met someone new.

Is free help real help for me?

Yes, free help is, but also remember that someone has taken the time to put that together.

If you are offering something in return, fantastic – free help is absolutely fine but just also respect someone's boundaries. If someone has said, you know actually at this point this is where I stop, don't keep pushing them. You've also got to trust that person is going to place their boundaries as well and trust that they are going to tell you where the boundary is. I'll probably just leave this person alone or if they offer you a service you get to decide whether you want to use that service or not and that's what I would take from that.

How shall I prepare for opportunities?

Just ask questions. I don't think can you prepare for opportunities. Know you can say yes to everything. I am very open-minded and I say yes to a lot of things and that's how I would prepare for opportunity. I always go into something thinking, what is my learning point? And when I reflect on something, I think what did I actually take away from that, even if it was a really complicated tough situation. So, I think every situation that you get into is an opportunity. Do you need to spend hours and hours preparing for it? If you only have someone's time for 10 to 15 minutes, don't overstep your welcome, prepare questions that you want them to answer and stick to that and be prepared to be open-minded about it. Listening is key and take away the learning points.

Which beginners' property books would you recommend?

I prefer listening to property podcasts. I also like that you can listen to podcasts while doing other things, like driving. Podcasts are people talking about real life situations, and that's far more interesting to me than reading a book that doesn't go into as much detail as I would like it to do. I absolutely love reading but I spend more time reading things about mindset and how I can help myself than I do about property investment.

Which property strategy should I follow?

Wow, that's a big question and I wonder if that's even the right question to be asking as a beginner. Here is what I say to all of my clients. You need to know what your end goal is in the first place, so where do you want to get to with property, and then work backwards from there.

What types of property do you actually want to invest in? Remember, a type of property is not a property strategy – too many people are pedalling that myth. If you're doing commercial that's a type of property, if you're doing HMO that's type of property, if you're doing service accommodation that's a type of property, it's not a strategy.

The strategy is the step-by-step process you take to get somewhere, and within that you've got time goals that you want to hit, and you've got other metrics that you want to hit at certain times. Get to the end goal and work back: how many properties do I need to buy in order to achieve that goal? What is then the metric of each of those properties? How much do I need to buy that property for, how much should that rental income be so that I can hit my net profit or target yields, and then how much money do I need in order to be able to buy that type of property and where am I going to get it from? Then I'd cash flow out the whole thing – so I look at my other assets and I think how can I manoeuvre around my money, my assets, my equity so that I can keep buying these properties.

That is a strategy and that will be personal to you and your role on the type of property you want to buy, so I can't tell you exactly what type of strategy is for you but I can tell you to put your blinkers on and write down what you want to achieve from property and then fill in the gap between where you are today and where you want to go. That is then a strategy that works for you.

How do I get the properties I want?

You go out and search the market for them. Phone agents, look on Rightmove, get out on foot, walk the streets. If you've got a target property that you're after, I would keep looking and looking and just get to know as many local agents in the area, be on Rightmove and all the property portals, get on local agents Facebook groups. I personally don't care whether they're off market or market – it doesn't really bother me – it's more about just getting deals, analysing them and then picking one that's right.

What kind of money do I need to get my first property?

I think £30,000 is a really nice sum of money. You could do it with £20,000 but £30,000 seems to be a good starting point.

How can I find people I can trust to give me the right guidance?

Gut instinct, keep asking around, keep looking for the right people. Some people are great, other people aren't. You don't have to be really humble and polite in this industry if someone's not like that to you, just please remember that you do need to be a bit assertive, but at the same time it's always gut, talk to people and see if you like them or not. If you don't, don't follow them, if you do, use their advice.

34. Paul Duval

About Paul

Paul started Cliftonvalley Property Limited in 2017 to invest in, buy, refurbish and hold property, and then Cliftonvalley Apartments in 2018, working with his son, Matt. They invest in Rent-to-Serviced Accommodation and provide training services and consultancy on SA systems. They also provide SA set-up and management services under Cliftonvalley Management hands-free for other landlords and investors, focused on corporate stays in Bristol. Using income generated from their management services and Rent-to-SA companies, they meet all outgoings and Paul is now concentrating on acquisition of redevelopment projects for SA, HMO and BTL to build up the Cliftonvalley 'owned' portfolio.

Paul has co-hosted the PPN Bristol Property Networking Event since 2018, along with Paul Bennett. They met on the Progressive VIP mentorship programme and share mutual aims to build their portfolios and companies further, and to share their experience and enthusiasm, in order to help others develop their property investment careers.

Presently, Paul is managing 28 Serviced Apartments with a £850k turnover and also personally owns a portfolio worth nearly £1.2m – comprised of two single lets, and one within the Cliftonvalley Property company, which has been refurbished and is ready to sell.

Based	Bristol
Investment location	Bristol, South Wales, Cheltenham & Gloucester
Strategies	• Serviced Accommodation • Rent to Serviced Accommodation • Serviced Accommodation Management, • HMO • Single Lets
Favourite sayings/ affirmations/mottos	• *'Whether you think you can,* or you *think you can't* – you're right' – Henry Ford • 'If you do what you always did, you will get what you always got' – Anonymous • 'Success is walking from failure to failure with no loss of enthusiasm' – Winston Churchill • 'Keep on Keeping on'
Three key learnings you would like to share with readers	• It will always take 50% longer than you think! • Property is a people business • Your network really is your net worth!

Job (if in a job previously)

Senior Project Manager in IT Networks and Telecommunications.

Why did you leave your job?

I left my long-standing career in 2019 to focus on my property businesses. Having project managed multi-million-pound projects with global teams in blue chip companies and government agencies as a contractor, I'd started to invest in buy-to-let property in 2013. I discovered the full potential of the many different streams of property income in 2017–2019 through Progressive Property's MSOPI weekend and then by making considerable investment in myself through courses and VIP mentorship with Progressive and others during that period.

What do you love about your life now?

I've really enjoyed networking and meeting people over the past three years since deciding on the full-time property path. I've met some lifelong friends and great contacts along the way.

Education, training, learning

Progressive Property's MSOPI weekend and then by making considerable investment in myself through courses and VIP mentorship.

Favourite books

- Robert T Kiyosaki, *Rich Dad, Poor Dad*
- Mike Michalowicz, *Profit First*
- Brian Tracy, *Eat That Frog!*

Contact details

Websites: www.cliftonvalleyapartments.co.uk

Linktree: https://linktr.ee/ppnbristol (for PPN Bristol)

Paul's Answers

How do I choose the right education, training and learning for me?

Start with defining your goals and what you're looking to do. Once that's done, I'd advise you get recommendations from people already doing what you're planning to do and who are ahead of you in that field. Find out what worked for them and what training they suggest for you, to help achieve your aim. There's lots of Facebook groups and lots of places online to get information on different training courses. I wouldn't go to any paid ones without doing something free from the same organisation, to see what you think of them. Then see what's available and what recommendations you hear for their more advanced training and go for that, if it meets your requirements.

What happens when I start learning and realise there's more I don't know than I do know, or that there's too much to learn?

I think whatever you do in life this will be the case, so I'm afraid you'll have to accept that. It's just a case of moving in the right direction by taking steps towards what you want to do. Take the pizza approach – eat a slice at a time. Don't worry about everything that's out there, just try and find out enough to get you started. You'll then be on the way towards your goals. Things will naturally progress from there as to whether you need more training, or more information, to get to the next level. It may be that at some stage mentorship and personal guidance becomes the best way forward after attaining a certain level.

How can I use my thoughts to help me do what I want?

Once you know what your goals are, you can think yourself through those goals on a daily basis. Some affirmations in the morning can help you realise how far you've progressed towards your goal, or visualise the way you expect to feel when you reach your goal. Visualisation is a powerful tool, so use it. Thinking of the thing that you're after on a consistent basis brings it closer!

How do I know which people to connect with to help me?

You need to connect with people that are doing, or have done, what you're planning to do, and those on similar journeys to you. I think whatever media it is that you're trying to connect with them on – whether it's a networking meeting, or social media, or online somewhere else – as long as you can see that they're doing what you want to do, it's worth connecting. Do a little bit of research about them perhaps, before you accept a connection. If they've got a Facebook profile and they're asking you to connect on there, then have a look at their profile and see if they're connected to people that you want to be associated with. Do a little bit of research, but do make lots of connections, grow your network in your field of interest and keep visible.

Is free help real help for me?

If possible, get the sort of free help that comes with a little bit of recommendation. There's one course that I'd recommend – I've been several times to the MSOPI (Multiple Streams of Property Income) weekend, which is a free event from Progressive Property. They do a great job of giving you information about a lot of property related topics, which can be very valuable.

How shall I prepare for opportunities?

Depends on the opportunity, but in general terms, do your research on the meeting or the opportunity that's coming up. If you're meeting somebody, find out a little bit about them, prepare some topics or questions you want to cover. Set your goals for the outcome of the meeting and work towards them.

Research is the best way to prepare for opportunities. Research the person you're meeting, the subject you're meeting about and research any business opportunity – for instance, due diligence on a property deal or purchase (values in the area, likely cost of renovations, previous sale history, how long on the market, something about the owner and reason for selling).

Which beginners' property books would you recommend?

Rich Dad Poor Dad by Robert Kiyosaki is a great book, though not specifically property; it's more mindset and approach to wealth and how to attain it, but a great book. *Start Now Get Perfect Later* by Rob Moore is also not specific to property, but it will certainly help you to stop procrastinating and get on with working towards your property goals. *No Money Down: Property Investing* by Kevin McDonnell, however, is very property specific, and a great guide. Kevin takes you through a lot of the property investing strategies in nice manageable sections.

Which property strategy should I follow?

The strategy you pick very much depends on what you want to achieve, but also it depends on how much income you've got, how much money you have available to invest, what savings you've got, and who you're connected with, or working with. What do you prefer to do on a day-to-day basis – do you want to get involved with tenants, or guests, on a regular basis, or do you want to set and forget? Or invest for a return and not get involved at all?

There are lots of different answers, depending on all those things and more. Once you know those things, you can work towards a strategy that both works for you and appeals to you. Find out about all of them and select what piques your interest and meets your needs!

How do I get the properties I want?

Decide what you want and then talk to agents, look online and chase them down. Get as many viewings as you can under your belt, build relationships with agents and get them to understand what you want. It may take a few visits, or discussions, or viewings, to explain to people what you're after.

Once you get a good estate agent, try and stick with them and keep in touch. Be specific on what you're aiming for – number of bedrooms, location, type of property. Once you've got all those nailed, then chase every one of those that you can find. Use Gumtree, Rightmove, Zoopla, Auction Houses, all the local agents, high streets. Save your searches and set notifications for similar properties from the websites.

What kind of money do I need to get my first property?

Sensibly to get started, you'd need maybe £5,000 or £10,000 to get started on a rent-to-rent property or a rent-to-SA property. With that amount of money, you've got enough to cover a couple of month's rent, some deposit, some money to tidy the property up, buy some furniture and set things up in terms of contracts. You can't really do it with no money (unless it comes from an investor, partner, or family member or friend).

How can I find people I can trust to give me the right guidance?

You need to research what they're offering and research people that have dealt with them in the past. Get recommendations and confirmation from your peers that they're potentially worth working with.

35. Paul Million

About Paul

Paul has been a landlord and developer for three decades. He's well-respected amongst his peers as a character and a sharer.

He runs two networking events: The Property Thing and Developers Network North East. Paul is a prolific investor across most strategies, with a perfectionist and fearless approach. He was 25 years 'on the tools'. Paul spends much of his time helping others, has a unique character and is author of some entertaining Facebook posts. He's one in a million – for sure! Paul's portfolio includes 80 properties including 20 HMOs, 60 BTLs, two Aparthotels (in planning) as well as renewable projects.

Based	Darlington
Investment location	Darlington
Strategies	BTL, SA, HMO, Light Industrial, Aparthotel, Commercial Conversion, Co-Working, Supported Living
Favourite sayings/ affirmations/mottos	• In every adversity lies the seed of a greater benefit • Shy Bairns Get Nowt
Three key learnings you would like to share with readers	• Have a network • Tell people what you do! • Never Give Up!

Age 50

Job (if in a job previously)

Royal Navy Technician, Sports & Workwear Supplier, Landlord.

Why did you leave your job?

To be a landlord/developer.

What do you love about your life now?

My network and capital appreciation.

Education, training, learning

- Commercial Conversions Mentorship. Progressive, Glenn Delve
- Newbuild Developer Mentorship, Whitebox
- Mark Stokes Equacademy Intro Course

Favourite books

- Stuart Goldsmith, *The Midas Method*
- Chris Voss, *Never Split The Difference*
- Jim Kwik, *Limitless*

Contact details

Email: paul.million@realpropertyuk.com

Paul's Answers

How do I choose the right education, training and learning for me?

There is a lot of generic overview in property. I think it depends on where you are in your journey, but a great overview would be to get to networking events and ask people that question. Some people have a strategy from the start, and they know what they want to do. Some, have a building that will only lend itself to certain strategies. Other people won't have a clue which way they want to go, but just know that property over a period of time is a great investment. So, in that respect it's generic to the person, but again you have to look at the menu and the way to find the menu is to get on Facebook and have a look at as many different places as possible. See where you feel like you fit in, and also ask other people who are above you on the ladder, what they would do. Get it all logged in a system of action – either by taking notes or whatever notes system you use but get it all in there with an action list. Also, get an accountability partner.

What happens when I start learning and realise there's more I don't know than I do know, or that there's too much to learn? want?

Well, being a seasoned property investor of more than 30 years, I sometimes feel like I know about 20% of what I should know, or what I could know. Don't let that hold you back because emotion, drive, vehemence, persistence are the most important factors – you don't need everything in place to start the journey.

How can I use my thoughts to help me do what I want?

By writing out your goals (see Chapter 9 of the *Midas Method*) and visualise them. When you visualise, have a pad next to you so that when your right brain starts chucking out lots of ideas you don't let that distract you.

How do I know which people to connect with to help me?

Networking events and Facebook and all of the other portals where you get involved in property. The ones to connect to are the ones that resonate with you.

Is free help real help for me?

Absolutely and help from:

- Other newbies
- People up the ladder
- Everywhere

You're a filter and it's up to you to have the intelligence and drive and motivation to filter out the stuff that you know isn't going to be useful to you and the stuff that is.

How shall I prepare for opportunities?

With open arms, a good filter and a good analyser spreadsheet. That's the way you want to go and by leveraging your network and asking questions of the people above you on the ladder.

Which beginners' property books would you recommend?

Property Magic by Simon Zutshi is a great one to start thinking about property, but also for opening your mind to creative dealings.

Which property strategy should I follow?

The one that feels most congruent to the amount of time that you've got to put into it, where you are in your actual career (whether that be your working career or your property career) and also what you feel confident to be able to tackle.

It took me to get to 35 buy-to-lets, before I could take the full-time jump into property. What I would have changed about my journey is that I would have done a couple of buy-to-lets that would have put me in my comfort zone at the time, but as soon as possible I would have moved up into the higher cash-generating strategies such as HMO and SA – because it's not as difficult as you think. It's fairly straightforward. Any property strategy is fairly straightforward, but you just have to be organised and disciplined in what you do, and with the information that you gather in order to implement your strategy.

How do I get the properties I want?

By believing that, 'You're worth it'. You have an aura, and the aura that you put out will help people create a genesis with you. If you put yourself out into the world and you put your aura out there and you deal with people on a professional and friendly basis, the deals will come to you. And always tell people what you do. Make sure you post anything that's going to help anyone else on the journey and as a result of that selling will definitely reward you.

Then you've got your normal stuff like Right Move and the Zoopla websites – you have to put your hardy heart into get results. You have to wear out the shoe leather and put the hard yards in and be able to spot opportunities as you walk down the street.

I have a terrible trait, which means that I have a problem with my legs – I can't walk past a decrepit property without thinking about how that property could be brought back into being. I wonder who owns it and then I ask some questions about that property because it's all on the Land Registry and the neighbours will know as well.

What kind of money do I need to get my first property?

You need enough money, and it depends on what strategy you do. I ended up with a flat recently from a lady where she actually gave me the flat – it's called a completion of deferred consideration. If you know someone and if they trust you, you can put the charge on a different building and have an unencumbered property in your name for no money whatsoever. But you might have to pay to refurb it and you will have to pay that person for that property at some point in the future, but that's quite a creative strategy. There are other ones like exchange of delayed completion and purchase lease options and things like that. So, you may not need as much money as you think, but you have to make sure that the deal works.

How can I find people I can trust to give me the right guidance?

Networking events. You're never more than one or two people away from the person you really need to speak to, and when you go to a networking event – if there's 50 people there – their network becomes your network if you ask the right questions and give out the right aura.

36. Paul Percival

About Paul

I have run a second-generation re-upholstery business in Caerphilly, South Wales for 30+ years and pretty much enjoyed every minute,

but over the last three years I have been steadily been building my property portfolio to a level where it now cashflows more than my than my day job.

Interestingly, when I look back on what I have achieved with property it doesn't seem I was that difficult especially when I compare the time and work the effort required on upholstery. For example, if I upholster a three-piece suite, I would probably get £450 profit, which may take me two days to achieve. On the other hand, if I purchase £120,000 house requiring a £30,000 deposit, I get roughly £300 profit per month, but the huge difference is I get paid this for life, so I don't mind putting the short-term effort in for the long-term gain. Plus, in my experience, every 15 years the property value can double while your debt will erode to a more manageable level. Property has been a real winner for me and it can be for you too. Good luck to all thinking of starting their property journey!

Based	South Wales, UK
Investment location	South Wales and beyond
Strategies	Buy-to-let; mixed use; commercial
Favourite sayings/ affirmations/mottos	Always think two years ahead
Key learnings you would like to share with readers	• Your debts always erode over time, so hang on in there, and start young. • Try to buy in a limited company so you can pass your properties down the generations.

Age 53

Job (if in a job previously

30 fabulous years in the re-upholstery game.

Why did you leave your job?

I am in transition.

What do you love about your life now?

The people you meet on your journey and freedom of choice.

Education, training, learning?

I listen to lots of free podcasts, and am an active member of NC Real Estate.

Favourite books

- Robert T. Kiyosaki, *Rich Dad, Poor Dad*
- Kevin McDonnell, *No Money Down*, and anything else by this author
- Any books by Rob Moore

THE 1ST PLACE.

Contact details

Website: lumapropertysolutions.com

Paul's Answers

How do I choose the right education, training and learning for me?

There are so many resources that are available on the internet. I think you should set aside some time to study each one and absorb what it's about. Then see which one applies to you, but I think it will depend on how much money you want to, or can, start with.

Some people walk into this with just a pound in their pocket, other people might have hundreds of thousands available, so obviously that dictates where you want to start.

What happens when I start learning and realise there's more I don't know than I do know, or that there's too much to learn?

I remember going back to 1985, my geography teacher said to me, 'I learn something every day', and I looked at him and I thought, well, he's a teacher, doesn't he know everything? But he openly admitted he didn't, which surprised me, and I think it's a brilliant mindset to have. I have witnessed exactly the same scenario even with famous property experts and gurus like Rob Moore – they put themselves in a position where they're still humble enough to recognise that they can still learn.

How can I use my thoughts to help me do what I want?

Well, if you think a lot about a certain situation or problem or business enterprise that you've got, I think you naturally work your way through the problem and find an outlet to be able to exercise what you have just learnt.

How do I know which people to connect with to help me?

I think through the numbers game. What you need to think about is going through a few mentors on a basic level to see which ones you connect with, but don't just listen to the first person that you see.

Is free help real help for me

Absolutely. I think free help is such a wonderful thing. As I said in the last question, you need to go through as many people as you can, and you'll find those very same people will give you a lot of free advice. There is also an abundance of podcasts to listen to, books, social media – you can spend days and days listening to mentors and not even commit yourself to engage in any conversation with them.

How shall I prepare for opportunities?

I think you need to prepare for opportunities by keeping an open mind and never have a shotgun opinion about somebody. Always listen fully to what they say.

Which beginners' property books would you recommend?

For beginners I would say Kevin McDonnell's book, *No Money Down Property Investing*. I find him very straightforward and he gives good clarity on what he's talking about.

Which property strategy should I follow?

Well, that depends on you because again, where do you want to start? How much money have you got? And how much time do you want to put into it? But you also need to study multiple strategies to see which one you feel suits you best, not just personally but financially.

How do I get the properties I want?

You go through the numbers by going to the estate agents, looking in windows. Also look on Rightmove, and Facebook marketplace is a good place for direct vendor purchases. There are just so many opportunities on the market right now. Yes, they are not cheap, but you get good returns from them if you play your cards right.

What kind of money do I need to get my first property?

If you want to buy your first property, my advice would be you need to have at least 25% of the value of the property that you are going to purchase.

How can I find people I can trust to give me the right guidance?

In your social circle you may have people that are property investors. Obviously, they'll be the first port of call, if you trust them and know them already. But what I tend to do is look for track records. I think if you approach people in networking events, they are normally quite open in what they have achieved already. Just be careful of people that just want money from you. Don't spend any money unnecessarily.

37. Paul Tinker

About Paul

Paul Tinker is a leading refurbishment expert, trainer, coach and mentor, as well as an award-winning developer, speaker, magazine columnist and author. A husband, proud dad of four and former soldier, Paul served 14 years as a Royal Engineer. After this, he trained as a bricklayer and now has over 15 years hands-on industry experience and is a PRINCE 2 project management practitioner. Paul's largest single project was £18 million. His refurbishment turnover is £300 million and he has successfully delivered over 3,000 projects nationally.

Based	North Lincolnshire (UK)
Investment location	Yorkshire and Humberside, Lincolnshire
Strategies	I am a trainer, coach and mentor in the refurbishment project management sector. I teach folk how to make more profit from their refurbishment projects using a repeatable system. I run a construction business that delivers those refurbishment services to the property space and more specifically Grade 2 listed refurbishment projects
Favourite sayings/ affirmations/mottos	• 'Do the fuckin' work' • 'Square metre rates are for dummies' • 'Quotes without a spec are a fuckin' guess' • 'Stop fuckin' wingin' it'
Key learnings you would like to share with readers	• All of our mistakes in life are the things that put us where we are right now, so for all of that I am truly grateful • There's nothing stronger than a person who's rebuilt themselves

Job (if in a job previously)

Former soldier, serving 14 years as a Royal Engineer; trained bricklayer, with over 15 years hands-on industry; project management.

Why did you leave your job?

Had enough of the corporate lifestyle and stress of work, so decided to go it alone.

What do you love about your life now?

Enjoys delivering training to property investors and trades; constantly pushing and challenging himself in order to grow and develop.

Education, training, learning

Served 14 years as a Royal Engineer; 15 years as a trained bricklayer; PRINCE 2 project management practitioner; ongoing project experience (largest project was £18million and has successfully delivered over 3,000 projects nationally).

Favourite books

- Napoleon Hill, *Think and Grow Rich*

- Anything by Byron Katie and anything by Ant Middleton
- Paul Tinker (my book!), *Refurbishment X – Projects Done Properly*

Contact details

Website: www.constructiontrainingacademy.com

Email: Info@constructiontrainingacademy.com

Paul's Answers

How do I choose the right education, training and learning for me?

Before education you need to decide on your strategy – your strategy first and education second.

What happens when I start learning and realise there's more I don't know than I do know, or that there's too much to learn?

That's always going to happen, and I see it in my own training business. When you've learned something, go and implement it. Otherwise you'll just get shiny penny syndrome and you'll be flicking off all over the place – different strategy for this, different course for this, next course, next course, next course. Always while studying, you're learning and you're implementing. Do one course, implement it, get the return on the investment you've put into the training and then move on to something else.

How can I use my thoughts to help me do what I want?

Your thoughts and beliefs will drive your actions and behaviours.

How do I know which people to connect with to help me?

Values. Aligning your values with a peer group – like anything else. You'll just know who you want to connect to because it's in your gut.

Is free help real help for me?

I think it is. The problem I have with free help is that the person receiving it doesn't value it, not the other way around. There is a difference between being valuable and being valued.

How shall I prepare for opportunities?

I don't think you can. I think you've got to know when it comes that it's an opportunity, take action and get after it.

Which beginners' property books would you recommend?

My one – *Refurbishment X – Projects Done Properly*.

Which property strategy should I follow?

That's a massive topic. If you're asking me personally – then it's anything that I can add value to.

How do I get the properties I want?

Put in the highest bid.

THE 1ST PLACE.

What kind of money do I need to get my first property?

You need access to finance. People have this belief that they have to have this money in the bank. It doesn't have to be, you just need to have access to it. If you know a relative that's got access, then you've got finance. The money's not in your bank, but you've still got the access to that finance.

How can I find people I can trust to give me the right guidance?

Same again, go with your gut.

38. Paula Bushnell

About Paula

I buy, refurbish and resell or rent residential properties in Essex. I transform tired properties, which the owner may have struggled to sell, into warm, safe, comfortable homes for local people. This is a win-win situation as it allows the seller to carry on with their lives, the property is improved and value added, homes are provided for local people, and myself and my investors get cashflow and/or capital value increases from the investment.

Based	Essex, UK
Investment location	Essex, UK
Strategies	Residential flips, Serviced accommodation (BRRR: Buy, Rent, Refurbish, Refinance)
Favourite sayings/ affirmations/mottos	• 'If you think you can or you think you can't, you are right' Henry Ford • Carpe diem
Three key learnings you would like to share with readers	• Take action every day. Action + Energy = Results. • All of the 'No Money Down' strategies taught by Kevin McDonnell. • By building a network of people who you know, like and trust, there will always be somebody who can help you solve queries and problems.

Job (if in a job previously)

Previously managed commercial property for NatWest Bank and Eon.

Why did you leave your job?

To follow my own property journey.

What do you love about your life now?

Freedom of being my own boss and leading the life I want to.

Education, training, learning?

Progressive Property VIP, No Money Down Mastermind, Deal Packaging Mastermind, Buy to Sell Bootcamp, Resonate Mastermind, Cashflow With Property Academy, NEBOSH Safety at Work, NRLA Accredited Landlord, British Horse Society Instructor.

Favourite books

- T. Harv Eker, *Secrets of the Millionaire Mind*
- Kevin McDonnell, *No Money Down Property Investing*
- Professor Steve Peters, *The Chimp Paradox*

THE 1ST PLACE.

Contact details

Email: pukkaproperty@gmail.com

Paula's Answers

How do I choose the right education, training and learning for me?

Everyone learns differently. Firstly, you've got to decide what format you want it in, (online, books or in the room) and then go to a recognised, reputable property training company and check up on them online – on Facebook and all of the online forums. Make sure you are going with a company that is going to do the best for you, and not scam you, because there are a few people out there that are taking money and not giving much value.

What happens when I start learning and realise there's more I don't know than I do know, or that there's too much to learn?

When you start learning such a huge subject such as property, it's probably going to be quite natural for most people to realise that there is more to it than they thought. But this is a good thing because it's opening your mind. You've really got to just drill down and find out which aspects you are interested in learning first and let that guide you.

How can I use my thoughts to help me do what I want?

Record them as the thoughts come into your head on a phone app or a little notebook, because sometimes thoughts can be quite fleeting and hard to get back at a later time.

You can maybe use something alongside this like the Miracle Morning Principle, which I use: I wake up an hour before I'm due to do any other activities and I run through all these thoughts and plans in my head, jot them down the night before, run through them in my Miracle Morning Hour and put them into a plan in the morning.

How do I know which people to connect with to help me?

I think you should:

- Watch them
- Follow them on social media, if you can
- Introduce yourself to them face to face at networking events
- Ask others what they think of them, if you can find someone you are happy to ask

Is free help real help for me?

Yes, it can often be, and there is a lot of free help out there that is very good. It may be in the form of A free discovery webinar and/or free downloads, and there are also some great YouTube videos and podcasts you could watch and listen to.

How shall I prepare for opportunities?

Be ready for them with as much education as you can get, and have your plans ready so that when an opportunity comes along you can recognise it and know how to act on it.

Which beginners' property books would you recommend?

Kevin McDonnell's *No Money Down* which explains all the different strategies that you can follow without having to use your own money, and *44 Property Secrets* by Rob Moore and Mark Homer – a really good one for beginners that explains everything.

Which property strategy should I follow?

Pick a strategy that will work in your area: you know your area and you've researched it so you can see what is likely to work and what is not. When you've drilled down to that much detail, pick a strategy that you feel passionate about because it's going to take all of your mental energy and emotions to get these deals through successfully. You can't try to follow a strategy that you're lukewarm about, so find out what works in your specified area and then pick a strategy that you a passionate about and also that is realistic from a financial point of view.

How do I get the properties I want?

Depends on what sort of properties they are, but usually with any property you are after it's by taking those daily actions to follow a plan, and then implementing that plan to a successful conclusion.

What kind of money do I need to get my first property?

Probably very little money, although you need a little bit. There are a lot of opportunities you can follow, where you can joint venture with somebody who puts money in, for example. It's going to be very little when taking on a rent-to-rent property. You can probably to do that from £3–£5,000 to set up – it doesn't have to be hundreds of thousands.

How can I find people I can trust to give me the right guidance?

Ask around, watch people online, see what they are doing, look at what they are posting and what kinds of projects they say they are successfully completing. Follow that up through people you know and trust.

39. Peter Wood

About Peter

Peter is an award-winning business consultant specialising in supporting, coaching and holding accountable business owners, executives and managers. He has experience of successful coaching delivery in a variety of industries but his niche is in getting property investors to overcome overwhelm and procrastination and take the necessary actions to achieve their goals.

Peter's property investments range from single lets to commercial to residential conversions, from refurbishments of character properties to construction of houses. He also helps investors and partners get excellent returns by using innovative strategies to secure and deliver profitable property deals.

Peter owns and runs a real estate agency with his son Joe. He also provides non-executive directorship services specialising in business development, sales, marketing, networking and property investment. Peter's goal is to help others towards financial and time freedom.

Based	Suffolk
Investment location	London, Suffolk, Yorkshire, Lancashire, Northumberland
Strategies	R2R; SA; BTL; BRR; lease purchase options; single lets; refurbishment; land; construction
Favourite sayings/ affirmations/mottos	• Focus • If you want something done, ask a busy person • You don't have to be perfect to start... but you do have to start to achieve anything
Three key learnings you would like to share with readers	• Know exactly why you are doing this • Chose a coach that you know like and trust who will guide you and keep you accountable • Focus and take action

Age 57

Job (if in a job previously)

Recruitment; life Insurance; IFA and mortgage advisor; bank and building society manager; Head of Marketing for a business loans firm.

Why did you leave your job?

Redundancy – so I took the leap to go self-employed.

What do you love about your life now?

The challenges; the networking and interaction; the opportunity to help others.

Education, Training, Learning?

- BA (Hons) Social Science

- Diploma in Performance Coaching (Business)
- Award in Business Advice – Small Firms Enterprise Development Initiative
- IOEE Level 3 Social Media Advertising and Promotion
- IOEE Level 2 Promotion of Products and Services through Social Media
- Association of Professional Coaches – Elite Performance Coaching Certification Masters
- FSA – Financial Planning Certificate III
- FSA – Certificate in Mortgage Advice and Practice
- Numerous Property courses and Masterminds

Favourite books

- Robert T. Kiyosaki, *Rich Dad Poor Dad*
- Kevin McDonnell, *No Money Down*
- Gary Keller, *The Millionaire Real Estate Investor*
- Curtis '50 Cent' Jackson, *Hustle Harder, Hustle Smarter*

Contact details

Email: Peter.wood@nightwood.ltd

Peter's Answers

How do I choose the right education, training and learning for me?

You've first of all got to consider three things,

- why you're going into property
- what you want to achieve
- what your goals are

because the education and training you choose is going to depend on this to start with.

If you don't think about that before you start, you'll end up buying courses on a willy-nilly basis, which many, many people do. They become course junkies and still can't get started because they think that they need more education.

If you can tailor your education to what you need because of what your goals are and what you want to achieve, you'll then be able to determine which is the correct provider for you, which is the correct person to associate with, and who are the best people to learn from.

There is so much learning you can get both for free and from various different sources but choosing somebody that you know, like and trust to deliver those will make a big difference to your journey. You can gain education but, frequently, you won't get somebody who will assist you in implementing that knowledge and for most of us that's something that is far, far more important. Having somebody who can coach you into implementation; to get rid of your overwhelm; to stop you procrastinating and make you take action.

What happens when I start learning and realise there's more I don't know than I do know, or that there's too much to learn?

You don't have to be perfect to start, you've got to start somewhere. If you start to get education and realise there's far more out there than you had anticipated in the first place, you've probably overcome the very first barrier that many of us have in investing in property because you've realised you can't know it all.

You will need specialist advice at times for different aspects of your property investments, because there will be legal situations legislative management of sites, contracts that you've got to put in place. You will make mistakes – we all make mistakes – but you'll be able to be making daily progress.

How can I use my thoughts to help me do what I want?

You've got to use your thoughts to do what you want; you've got to think things through.

If you've gone in without thinking things through, you've got no idea of where you want to go, so how do you know you've achieved anything?

All of those thoughts are very good things, but it might well be that you need to bounce those thoughts off somebody else, so that they can assist you in determining the correct way forward. Writing them down will also make a difference, in terms of what your thoughts are, because your mind will move from one point to another automatically as your thoughts change. So, having them written down will definitely assist you. Then, review your thoughts, and what you agreed to do to take action against that thought. Ask yourself, did you take that action and what was the outcome? And what do I need to do next? Keep doing this; rinse and repeat. You've got to use these thoughts.

How do I know which people to connect with to help me?

You don't, until you connect with them and speak to them and work out whether they're somebody that you feel confident in. You'll need to get to know them, build relationships with them and only then can you know whether there the right people to take you forwards.

You can jettison people afterwards, that's not an issue. And I'm not suggesting that you accept every single friend request that you might ever get on Facebook either, because you undoubtedly get some strange ones along the way. So not necessarily accepting everybody as a new connection is a good rule of thumb.

Consider, too, how you can help them, which will actually help you. If you can answer the question, 'What am I going to do for them?', you're going to be far better off in terms of building a network and making progress. They'll be looking at it from the point of view of 'How does this person help me?' So, if you've got an answer for them, you could be interesting, and if you're looking for finance this could prove very valuable. Work out your own answer as to why you benefit them, and if you benefit them there's a good chance that they'll benefit you.

Is free help real help for me?

Any help's help; any advice will assist you. It is down to you to decide what advice you want to take. You don't want to take all free advice, but somebody suggesting something to you via free help can very much take you forwards, and make you think about things in a different way.

I personally had decided exactly what strategies I wanted to follow, and they were based on my own availability of time. I wanted to be fairly hands-off; I didn't really want to be in Serviced Accommodation or HMOs, I didn't have the knowledge to get involved in major refurbishments. However, along the way, I realised I have other skills that I can offer to other people to help take them forwards. My own giving free help has really assisted my journey, and other people offering free help has been great. There is value in free help, and there can be very significant value in help that you've paid for.

How shall I prepare for opportunities?

I would suggest that the first thing to do is to make sure that you are open-minded as to what an opportunity is. There's a famous diagram that says, 'Opportunity is nowhere', which changes to, 'Opportunity is now here' just by slightly repositioning those same words, with spaces in different places. Be prepared for opportunities, be conscious of what somebody might be bringing to you, network extensively, know what you can add to an opportunity, and then you'll be prepared for opportunities that otherwise you might not have seen. I didn't used to be open-minded about opportunities and said no to a number of them in the past. Now, I tend now to say, 'Yes, what's the question?' or 'OK, I am interested in a project, but what's the project?' I say I'm interested, then do my due diligence and check it's viable.

Which beginners' property books would you recommend?

I wouldn't necessarily say it needs to be a property book. There are some great books that are often used by property people, such as Kiyosaki's *Rich Dad Poor Dad* and 50 Cent's book about hustling. One property coach book I benefited very much from reading is Kevin McDonnell's *No Money Down*, but I don't think they need to be specific property books, general business books will assist you far more when you're starting out.

Which property strategy should I follow?

This very much depends on,

- what it is that you want to achieve
- why you're investing in property
- what your goals are
- what your start point is, including your level of knowledge and experience

For example, somebody who has owned their own house for 15 years and has inherited another house with a value of £300,000, might follow a very different strategy from somebody who's always rented their house and has been in an industrial job. But an even bigger influence on which strategy is correct is knowing *what* you want to do and *why* you want to do it, as well as also knowing what you bring to the table. It's very much horses for courses what's the right strategy for an individual person.

How do I get the properties I want?

First thing I would be inclined to ask, is what properties do you want because that's going to make a difference to how you get them. Then you'll find them by

- building your network

THE 1ST PLACE.

- talking to people
- talking to estate agents
- talking to other property developers
- knocking on doors of people selling houses
- going to property meetings and chat to people about what it is that you're looking for and what have they got available
- talking to property sourcers who could put things in front of you that you might then be interested in
- getting more technical and use online systems to identify plots so you can gain planning consents and get an uplift on the value of the plot whether or not you go through with the construction of the project

What kind of money do I need to get my first property?

The amount of finance you've got available to you can make a difference to what strategies you can achieve. If you're a newbie in property and need a lot of finance for a big project, people aren't going to trust you because you've no experience at all of the industry. However, if you were in a Joint Venture partnership with people that have done it before and you happen to be the accountant, you could be in a wholly different situation because you're bringing something to the party.

Most of us need to start smaller; we might we lucky and have built up a pot of cash through savings or inheritance, or maybe we've gone through a divorce and ended up with a small cash pot. Or you might have a cash value from previous company pensions which can be loaned and or used within your own property journey, because now as a director of a company you can use your previous frozen company pensions to invest.

How much cash you need is going to depend on which strategies you want to perform in; even supposedly low-entry cash strategies, such as rent-to-rent or property sourcing, will need some element of investment in the first instance. People will say that you don't need any money, somebody always needs some money from somewhere even if it's not their money. There are all sorts of different sources of money and the more that you build up knowledge, experience, reputation and a name for yourself in the industry will make a difference as to where that cash will come from and at what rate you can borrow it.

How can I find people I can trust to give me the right guidance?

Network. Speak to lots of people, build relationships, don't try and do business straight away. Take the time to build those relationship and get to know people, and once you've done that you'll automatically gravitate towards the right people. At times you might find you'll make mistakes. I myself have had a business partner that proved to be not the right person for me... but you take the learning from that to go forward into whatever it is you do next.

40. Ranjit Seehra

About Ranjit

Ranjit is a Chartered Civil Engineer based in Derby, UK and has over 30 years' experience within property and construction. After gaining some 'formal' property training in 2015 he and his business partner invested in single lets and HMOs. Ranjit left his corporate life in 2019 and alongside property investing he has helped over 600 people and families with their property projects through his design consultancy, SREAR Design & Consulting. He offers mentorships to ensure businesses set off and grow successfully.

Based	Derby, UK
Investment location	East Midlands
Strategies	To own property including single lets, HMOs and commercial property.
Favourite sayings/ affirmations/mottos	Shoot for the stars, and even if you miss you will still land up amongst the stars!
A key learning you would like to share with readers	Understand your risk

Age 55

Job (if in a job previously)

Chartered Civil Engineer.

Why did you leave your job?

The timing was right to go it alone!

What do you love about your life now?

The time and freedom to do random things!

Favourite Books

- Rob Moore, *Life Leverage*
- Mark Homer and Glenn Delve, *Commercial Property Conversions*
- Sun Tzu, *The Art of War*

Contact details

Email: ranjseehra@gmail.com

Ranjit's Answers

How do I choose the right education, training and learning for me?

Short question long answer. What's best for an individual will depend on their present level of knowledge, experience and, therefore, the gaps that they need to fill. It's a very open-ended question and is really down to the individual. For example, if you're starting out in property and have no indication at all, just pick up any books or videos on single lets. These are the bread and butter of the industry. This is when you buy a property and rent it out to a family and you have very little maintenance.

So, get to understand what that process involves. Many people are happy with just doing single lets in their portfolio – you might have a landlord of 15 years with, say, 20 properties behind him or her actually needs no education because they are happy with their single lets. They have got it mastered.

It will depend on what your goals are, and gaps are in your knowledge, and where you want to be but yeah, it's tricky – it's a long question or a short question with a long answer. It all goes back to identifying what is it you want to do. Very much like in a menu in a restaurant where you can taste everything, you got to taste a little bit of everything and then decide where you want to start.

What happens when I start learning and realise there's more I don't know than I do know, or that there's too much to learn?

It's a fork in the road scenario. So, you can either persevere, learn a bit more and take action, or decide – and this is genuine because I have met many people who have decided to do this – decide 'this is not for me', and stop. Not everyone can be an entrepreneur.

It's a red pill, blue pill choice. You've got these two choices and you've got to make the choice. That doesn't mean that's the choice for ever as you can always come back later. If you choose to persevere, then persevere hard and if you choose to stop and do something else that's OK.

There is no right or wrong answer, no single track through the forest, and I have known many people through doing mentoring together and they have decided that actually property isn't for them – they have gone back to a day job and are quite happy doing that. So, all decisions are good decisions at the time they are made.

How can I use my thoughts to help me do what I want?

Thoughts alone are not going to get you anywhere. Sorry if it sounds a bit harsh but everything starts with a thought and idea, but it's the turning of that idea into an action, into something productive that's going to get you anywhere. So, meditate by all means and have positive thoughts and change your way of thinking to be, as I say, forward looking not backward looking, and if you can do that then you've got to take action, you've got to do something. Whatever it might be, however small, you've got to get up and do it.

How do I know which people to connect with to help me?

Ok, so at the moment a lot of people are connecting online and it's a fairly safe environment, so connect with as many people that appear to have the knowledge that you're looking for and chat with them.

When you are meeting face to face it's a different scenario. You can pick up more from mannerisms, from the way they behave in public – their character and personality come out. So, go with your gut feeling there as well. Everyone's different and there is always something you can learn from someone, meet as many people as you like and, at some point, the best people for you to work with will come out.

Start with a gut feeling, but if it feels right don't just jump straight in, there is a process here. Don't commit until you know almost everything lines up and you're happy. It's a mixture of personality, character and, I suggest, finding out if they have dealt with any crises. That's the telling point about someone – how did they deal with their last crisis? It's a great question to ask someone to see have they got the experience etc that can help you.

Is free help real help for me?

Yep, there is lots of free help out there and I think you should take advantage of all of it. Check, however, if it's just a sales pitch – you've got to differentiate between real help and sales pitch help and be very careful with that.

How shall I prepare for opportunities?

Opportunities are always there and you will only see them when you are prepared. So, how do you prepare? It's a case of taking little steps... If it's the first property you want to get into, just get out there and do viewings. One easy first step – get on Rightmove. There is no right or wrong solution here. Talk directly to vendors, but if you're new just get out there, book viewings and go and see them.

Also, go to auctions. There is an auction at least once a month in most towns and cities. Go and see what that smells, tastes and feels like. Immerse yourself in the experience because actions are required and you've got to do something. Simply do little bit of reading and then go and do it.

Which beginners' property books would you recommend?

Anything by Rob Moore and Mark Homer. Especially, *44 Secrets of Property Investing* and *Multiple Streams of Property Income*. They've written three or four solid property books in this field and also about 10 or so Mindset books. Just get one a week or one a fortnight and get on with it.

Which property strategy should I follow?

So, the strategy will depend on whether you want cash flow now, or capital growth later, or something in between. If you want cash flow, then you've got to acquire a property and get it cash flowing, so it may be simple single lets or one or two HMOs. You can buy them or get them on a rent-to-rent basis. These are options that are available for quick cash flow.

If you're less worried about cash flow and more about capital growth, you may want to get into developments or conversions where you are creating new assets – a lot more risky and a lot more experience needed, but with the right team of people around it can be done.

How do I get the properties I want?

Pay over the odds for them? OK, if you want the property that you want then, yeah, you've got to be prepared to pay more than the asking price. As simple as that. But if you want to do it as a business then you've got to do your analysis – the property you may want, or the property you need, or the property that may give you the best return might be three different things.

Property investing has got to be done semi-dispassionately and looked at as a business, so look at the numbers, and only offer the right number for that property in the condition it's in. People talk about properties being below market value because they are a bit tired and need some money spending on them, or someone may be in a very difficult situation and needs to move on, so they're are distressed sales or semi-distressed sales. Do you want that property? A new beginner may not want a property that's tired and needs a lot of work on it, but that is usually actually the best property for you as an investor. So, it's not about want, it's about how the numbers stack up.

What kind of money do I need to get my first property?

The minimum you would need to buy is the value of the deposit – and that is on the basis that you can get a loan for the balance. If you were doing a rent-to-rent deal you may not need a lot of money at all. Let's talk numbers here. Currently a small terrace property may cost, say £100,000 and there are still a few available here! If it needs no work on it, you need £25,000 deposit plus stamp duty and legals, say £30,000. You might persuade someone to rent you a property that you can then legally sub-rent on or sublet on, say as an HMO, and there's a margin there you may offer them. This could be £500 per month – so it's quite a large number – the main thing is you're trying to acquire or take control of a property that you can then leverage into a cash flow asset.

How can I find people I can trust to give me the right guidance?

You've just got to get out there and meet people – whether that's virtually, through social media, webinars or physical face-to-face network meetings. Get out there and meet people and then use your radar to pick the good ones from the bad ones. Look at what knowledge and experience they have and keep the personality separate from that. Also, once you've got a credible person there are people that they know, etc., so you're going through references and recommendations.

41. Richard Stone

About Richard

Richard is a multi-award-winning businessman, TED speaker and podcaster, as well as a contractor and developer, renowned for both his results and his sense of humour.

With experience in business, construction, leadership and management spanning decades, and as a former Supplier of the Year, his knowledge extends beyond just construction. Richard also works with others to maximise their profits and is highly regarded for his ability to dispense insightful no-nonsense advice. He is also respected for his huge work ethic and commitment to his own and other's personal development.

Richard is a much-respected coach, mentor and sought-after public speaker as well as being a Director of World Game Changers CIC. From small single unit BRRR projects with profits of £40k+ to huge decent schemes for National Social Housing providers, Richard has delivered thousands of projects in Residential Commercial, Industrial, Education, Healthcare, Government, and Military sectors totalling in excess of £100 million and generated tens of millions in profits, while creating homes where people can feel warm, safe and dry.

Based	Flitwick, Bedfordshire
Investment location	Hertfordshire, UK
Strategies	Flips, conversions and new builds
Favourite sayings/ affirmations/mottos	• Skillset without mindset, equals upset
Three key learnings you would like to share with readers	• Start NOW. Get perfect later • Always be conscious of your mental health • A thought is just that, it's neither true or false and it's a matter of choice to believe it or not

Age 44

Job (if in a job previously)

Contracts Director

Why did you leave your job?

To set up our own company

What do you love about your life now?

Choice

Education, training, learning

- Multiple MSOPI
- Progressive Masterclass
- Expert Speaker Academy

THE 1ST PLACE.

- Commercial Conversions
- Deal Packaging M/C
- I work with 4 coaches
- On Toastmaster's Pathways for public speaking
- Achieved MCIob
- Belong to multiple Mastermind groups

Favourite books

- David Goggins, *Can't Hurt Me*
- Marcus Sherdian, *They Ask You Answer*
- Mathew Syed, *Rebel Ideas*

Contact details

Website: www.richardmstone.co.uk

Linktree: https://linktr.ee/richardstone

Email: rs@stonecontracts.com

Richard's Answers

How do I choose the right education, training and learning for me?

The first thing is to understand which training company feels right for you. How do you like to learn? What's your preferred learning style – online or in the classroom? Do you like to read books or do you prefer to listen audio?

If you're someone who is completely new to property investing then you need to start with a training course that's going to give an overview of the whole industry – so you become educated about what the different strategies are. Then once complete, decide which works best for you – not only a strategy that will serve your needs, but also excite you because you've got to enjoy doing it. Then find out some more about that and look at other complementary skills around property, which might make you want to learn to succeed in property even more.

What happens when I start learning and realise there's more I don't know than I do know, or that there's too much to learn?

Firstly, remember, every day's a school day. I start every day by telling myself I know nothing, and I need to learn. This opens my mind to see lessons in things that otherwise I might miss. More strategically in relation to property, work out what you want to learn and then go find the best mentors or tutors on that subject.

For me, education is my highest regarded value and I'm a firm believer that you can never learn too much. So, work out what you want to know, establish what the gaps are in your knowledge and then build a plan to go out and get the training over the course of a period of time – *not* in one go, because otherwise you'll end up just utterly overwhelmed.

How can I use my thoughts to help me do what I want?

By understanding how the brain works. Get an understanding of neuro-linguistic programming and brain science, so you actually understand the power of thoughts and what thoughts actually represent. Not all thoughts serve you. Not all thoughts are relevant. A thought is just a thought – it's not real, you don't have to accept it. We have about 3,000 thoughts per hour, so it's a choice whether we hold onto them or let them pass. One of our biggest problems as human beings, is the fact that we are all limited to self-limiting beliefs.

How do I know which people to connect with to help me?

I'm a massive believer in the power of triangles, so ask other people what they do, listen to understand them and then succinctly explain what you require. Be open and honest about your experience or lack of it, show up as who you are and be open to have a conversation with anybody.

Is free help real help for me?

Free help can be real help, there's no reason why it can't. There can be tremendous value in free help, but if you're getting help from someone, I would try to find a way to check out what you're being told, as well as have a bit of a think about what the other person's motivation is.

How shall I prepare for opportunities?

You can't prepare for opportunities, other than ask yourself who you are, what your values are, what your mindset is and what your strength and weaknesses are. There's a really good phrase that applies here – 'Don't prepare to be ready, get ready.' So, always be ready no matter where you are. You don't know who you might bump into.

Recently, I was having a conversation when I was on a retreat with a young lad that I mentored about doing some work experience on one of our sites, and his mum asked whether I built property, told me she was an investor and asked if we could have a chat. It's about not preparing to get ready, it's about always being ready.

Which beginners' property books would you recommend?

There are a couple, by Rob Moore and Mark Homer, *Beginners Property Secrets* and *Multiple Streams of Property Income.*

Which property strategy should I follow?

Wow, that's a massive question! I think you've got to do something that serves your needs and that takes you out of your comfort zone – not to the point that you're overwhelmed – but so you're pushing yourself towards your goal.

How do I get the properties I want?

By working out a strategy that's going to work for you, and that's different for everybody. Some people have got many strategies they are working on, or with. I mean we've got three different strategies that are different for different streams we work with. We've got one strategy we work with for new build opportunities, one for trying to find properties we are going to do flips on and one that we do conversions with. It's about working out what's going to work for you. Some people would be absolutely aghast at the thought of sending out 100 letters on a direct to vendor campaign, other people would be up for it. It's a case of working out what's actually getting you the results. But test, tweak and track what you're doing, so you can actually manage whether its working for you.

What kind of money do I need to get my first property?

That massively depends on what your strategy is going to be. You could get an option agreement on a piece of land for a £1, or you could put that through planning and get £150,000 – £200,000 planning to go on that. You don't necessarily need loads of money. You could do rent-to-rent where you're not putting down a tremendous amount of money. There are lots of ways of using creative finance to do no-money-down deals, which can give people seriously big incomes.

How can I find people I can trust to give me the right guidance?

By attending networking events and looking at stuff people are doing online – not just the content those people are putting out there, but also at other people's responses to that content and how that person then responds to them.

42. Rick Cusimano

About Rick

Rick has overseen the purchase, refurbishment or conversion of 50+ houses for himself and his clients, including BRR single lets, HMOs and Commercial to Residential and New Build developments. With his wife and business partner Sophie, they have also grown a successful in-house letting agency. Rick also mentors investors who are looking to grow their property businesses.

Based	Derbyshire
Investment location	Chesterfield
Strategies	BTL, HMOs, Commercial to Residential, New Build
Favourite sayings/ affirmations/mottos	• If a job's worth doing, it's worth doing right!
Three key learnings you would like to share with readers	• Tell people what you do • Aim higher than you dare • Get started!

Age 40

Job (if in a job previously)

MD of a software house.

Why did you leave your job?

To pursue a new challenge in property.

What do you love about your life now?

Own boss, passive income.

Education, training, learning

Progressive Property, books, research.

Favourite books

- Robert Kiyosaki, *Rich Dad Poor Dad*
- Rob Moore and Mark Homer, *Property Investing Secrets*
- Rob Moore and Mark Homer, *Multiple Streams of Property Income*

Contact details

Website: www.dovedaleproperty.co.uk

Rick's Answers

How do I choose the right education, training and learning for me?

There is a little bit of chicken and egg in that question. To know exactly what training is best for you depends on where you're at, what you're trying to achieve and how you're trying to do it.

I think to understand what the right training is depends on what training they've had already. Are they aware of what property strategies work in their area, or their chosen area, and do they have all the knowledge about that chosen property strategy? If not, then that will be the next training I would suggest somebody take.

What happens when I start learning and realise there's more I don't know than I do know, or that there's too much to learn?

I think that's a very common situation to find oneself in. I think we're all guilty of under-estimating sectors we don't understand, and once we start learning more about a certain sector or topic, we realise it's a lot bigger than we thought. That's the case in any sector you know – we all think we're doctors from a five-minute Google search, but the reality is to really, really understand the medical field takes years and years of learning, constant training and up-skilling.

It's true of any sector that the more you learn about a sector, the more you realise you don't know about it. I wouldn't be daunted. You don't have to understand every facet of property to get into property, or every element of business to get into business. You just have to understand enough to get started, and then understand what the next most important thing to learn is. Don't be put off from discovering that a topic you've chosen is bigger than you thought. Some of the best things I've done have proven to be more challenging than I thought before I started them, but that's part of the reward – part of the win is learning about that new topic.

How can I use my thoughts to help me do what I want?

This question really leads on to the idea of mindset. Having the right frame of mind is not only beneficial; it's essential to achieving anything.

Take for instance somebody trying to start a new hobby or a new diet or a new routine. Having the right frame of mind, having the right goals, having the right reasons for those goals and being satisfied in their mind that they want to set up a routine, helps them to be accountable to that routine. It is 100% a mind task and a large part of what people talk about when they talk about mindset is getting the steps, the plan and the strategy in place. They consolidate the suggestions from people, consolidate training they've had, understand the situation they're in, and it gets them in the right frame of mind about what the next steps are.

How do I know which people to connect with to help me?

Speak to people and connect with everybody. Some people will really resonate with you and some people will just be acquaintances. The people you really resonate with either become friends, business partners, mentors or clients.

Is free help real help for me?

There are lots of free resources out there and there's lots of kind people happy to share some free advice to help you along on your journey. There are limits to how much free advice you might be able to get from somebody, and it can be very difficult to consolidate lots of free resources together into a cohesive sort of training pack, so I'd bear that in mind. It might take longer for you to get the same information, or it might be more disjointed and fragmented if it's come from lots of different sources. Ultimately, it'll still help you to form an idea or guide you on your next steps, but perhaps not as quick as paid resources might.

How shall I prepare for opportunities?

Opportunities present themselves whenever you take action. The more people you speak to, the more things you do, the more places you go to, the more opportunities seem to come up. To prepare yourself for opportunities, simply get out there and do something, meet people and take action.

Which beginners' property books would you recommend?

- Rob Moore and Mark Homer, *How to Make Cash in a Property Crash*
- Robert Kyasaki, *Rich Dad Poor Dad* – is a great one for getting your mindset around the idea of investing and passive income

Which property strategy should I follow?

That depends entirely on the individual, what their other income streams are, what their goals are, what part of the country they're in and what their chosen investment area is. There is no one answer for everybody – it depends on the individual and what they're trying to achieve.

How do I get the properties I want?

I'm assuming this question refers to investment properties. I would accumulate investment properties over time and use the buy, refurbish, and refinance strategy to buy them and grow a portfolio.

What kind of money do I need to get my first property?

It depends on the area that you're looking to invest in. In our area an average purchase price for a house that maybe doesn't need a lot of work would be say £95,000. So, 25% deposit on that will be around £25,000 (by the time we include stamp duty and solicitor fees). That's how much money you need to buy a property the traditional way, if you're trying to add value, then you might need to pay a bit extra for refurbishment. You might not need any money if you can raise the finance from family or friends, or even a bridging product.

How can I find people I can trust to give me the right guidance?

You need to try and deal with people you know, like and trust. They've got a proven track record, they've taken the steps you're looking to take, they resonate with you, you have things in common and your values are aligned – that's the most important thing.

43. Rochelle Gilburn

About Rochelle

Rochelle Gilburn is a mum of two and a multiple business owner. She started her property sourcing business in January 2020, right before lockdown, but that gave her time to step back, build her knowledge and confidence, and get ready to take on the world.

Since then, she has refurbed 12 properties at the time of writing, begun to build her own rental portfolio and helped investors to build theirs. Property is giving her the freedom to spend quality time with her family, while earning an income.

Based	South Yorkshire
Investment location	South Yorkshire
Strategies	BTL, flips, sourcing
Favourite sayings/ affirmations/mottos	It's so important to have a strong mindset
Three key learnings you would like to share with readers	• Small actions each day count – they add up and get the momentum going • Give yourself time to rest, you deserve a break • You are exactly where you should be right now

Age 33

Why did you leave your job?

I'd been there for 14 years and I felt like I needed to escape.

What do you love about your life now?

The freedom.

Education, training, learning

The Property Protégé with Paul McFadden

Favourite books

- Paul McFadden, *Property Protégé*
- Professor Steve Peters, *The Chimp Paradox*
- Tony Robbins, *Unleash The Power Within*
- T. Harv Eker, *Secrets of the Millionaire Mind*

Contact details

Website: www.rochellegilburn.com

Email: Contact@gilburninvestmentgroup.com

Rochelle's Answers

How do I choose the right education, training and learning for me?

I think a lot of it's about how you learn. I like sitting in a room and listening to somebody teach me. I learn really well like that. If I was given a series of YouTube videos to watch, I don't tend to take very much in and I find myself drifting off. I much prefer learning something in person, to be able to ask questions if I need to, then have the time to take in that information and digest it.

I know other people learn better from reading books, or from watching something and then being able to go away and watch it again over and over. I think it's worth asking:

- What type of learner are you?
- Who offers that product to you?
- What do you want to learn?
- Do you want a broad subject? (So you can decide which route you want to go in property or do you want something specific?)
- Do you just want to do something specifically? (Perhaps a Serviced Accommodation course or specifically an HMO course and learn deep on that one topic?)

What happens when I start learning and realise there's more I don't know than I do know, or that there's too much to learn?

Even the most experienced people don't know everything about a topic. There's always more to learn. I think it's about not getting overwhelmed by how little you know, but being proud of how much you do know, and be motivated to learn more. I remember the first investor call I had. I was so nervous and anxious, then I got on the call, and he was asking me questions and I was answering the questions. I realised I actually knew more that I gave myself credit for. The more I talked about it, the more I realised, 'Oh, yeah, I do know what I'm talking about'.

How can I use my thoughts to help me do what I want?

I did a Mind Power course by John Kehoe. It's a lot about focusing your mind affirmation, visualisations, mindset, weeding out all sorts of negative thoughts and replacing them with positive thoughts. It's about remembering that what you're thinking is powerful, so you need to be kind to yourself.

How do I know which people to connect with to help me?

There are a lot of people in property on social media. But sometimes you never know how much somebody is doing. I know early on in my journey, because I was so successful on social media, people thought I was further ahead in my journey than I was. Social media can be quite deceptive.

I'm a very trusting person, so I tend to trust people until they give me a reason not to. That's not always the best way to be. I'd say connect with people who are doing things you can visually see. You can see that they're doing refurbs, that they're out there doing property. You've just got to talk to people and give them a chance. You never know what you're going to learn. You might learn something from somebody who's been in property a few months, or you might learn something from someone who's been in property for years and years. I think everybody has different value to add from different points of view.

Is free help real help for me?

I think some people genuinely just want to be helpful, and then there are other people who want something out of it. But if it helps you and it helps them, then it's a win, win situation.

How shall I prepare for opportunities?

You need to do the work, learn, take those small actions and steps every day and an opportunity will come, and you'll be prepared for it. It's just learning. You don't always know when the opportunities are going to come and what they're going to be. Be open to the opportunities. Chase some opportunities but wait for others to land too.

Which beginners' property books would you recommend?

My mentor is Paul McFadden and his property books are really good.

- *Your Property Jumpstart* – is a general overview of getting started in property mainly down the line of having a sourcing business.
- *Property Success Mindset* – in this book he shares the things you need to learn to have a strong mindset in the property world and why you need to have a strong mindset. Then he did another one which is all about the marketing – all three are very good
- Steven Green, *Safe as Houses*. This book is a beginner's guide to property.

Which property strategy should I follow?

That's a personal choice. I source property for investors, but then I'm also building my own portfolio and doing flips as well. There are a lot of good strategies out there that I'd love to get started on – Serviced Accommodation is one example, but I think it's important to stay focused. Once I've built the sourcing company to the size that I want it, then I can move on to doing Serviced Accommodation. I don't necessarily think the strategy is the important thing – the important thing is to stay focused on that strategy and not hop around from one to another.

How do I get the properties I want?

Make sure you're viewing the properties that you want and that you're putting in the offers. Negotiation skills are always good to have, but also build relationships. A lot of the best deals I've had have come from estate agents that I've built relationships with. They bring the deals to me before they bring them to other people. By doing that, you've got access to a lot more deals and a lot more properties.

What kind of money do I need to get my first property?

If you're buying the first property for yourself, you'll need a 25% deposit if it's a buy-to-let. That's one mistake a lot of people make. They think they can do a 10 or 5% deposit like you can for a residential, but you need the 25% deposit. You also need the stamp duty (so it's a bit more than you'd pay if you were buying your first residential property), solicitor's fees, any refurb costs and then it depends on your strategy as well. Are you going to refurb it and then sell it on? Are you going to rent it out?

You're best having a bit of a contingency fund as well while you're refurbing it. You're going to pay council tax, gas, electricity and water bills. I know those are the things that sort of surprised me in the early days – I'd not considered working them into my figures.

How can I find people I can trust to give me the right guidance?

I think it's doing due diligence on the person to make sure they come recommended from other people and that other people have worked with them. A lot of the time you've got to trust your intuition about a person and listen to your gut instinct.

There's also a lot of research you can do if you look at Company House to see what businesses they've got, check out their social media channels, talk to people who know them or have worked with them. I'd say those are your main things, but make sure you're protecting yourself with agreements over any sort of charges.

44. Sarah Harding

About Sarah

I've always been a people person – I really enjoy meeting new people and hearing about their background and experiences. I'm motivated by working with others to achieve a common goal or to help them resolve a problem or challenge. Property raises challenges every day! If I can use what I've learnt so far to help others get on in this world, then I'm all the happier!

In the last few years we have built an HMO portfolio worth £1.5 million with a monthly rent role of £13k per month. In the same time, we have sold property of just over £1 million with profit of £400k.

Based	Brentwood, Essex
Investment location	Essex and Stoke-on-Trent
Strategies	HMOs, Flips & Commercial Conversions
Favourite sayings/ affirmations/mottos	What you focus on grows, so focus on the positive!
Three key learnings you would like to share with readers	• Identify your 'why', then make a plan to achieve it. You don't have to have a 5-year plan at the start, but a 6–12 month one is essential. Stay focused by goal setting to keep you on track and recognise your achievements. Celebrate your wins – especially the small ones! • Be accountable – if you can't be accountable to yourself, find someone to buddy with and keep each other accountable. Networking is essential to building relationships with like-minded people who will welcome support and be happy to share experiences. • Invest in yourself – we never stop learning new things, new ways of thinking or approaching challenges. When you are running your own business a growth mindset is essential to success. Celebrate the investment you make in training, coaching, mentoring and networking to enhance your skills and broaden your thinking – it will pay you back in dividends!

Age 44

Job (if in a job previously)

Project Manager specialising in finance transformation and change projects for large corporates in banking, financial services and property industries, plus worked on a two-year transformation programme for local government.

Why did you leave your job?

I still do the 'day job' on a part-time basis to give our family stability, particularly in the current climate. I've built a strong network in the city over the years, which I am thankful for as this enables me to work with talented people who are also my friends.

What do you love about your life now?

I have more flexibility now to balance family and work, which is really important to me. With a young family of three lively boys it's really important that we are able to be there for them and enjoy life!

There are so many opportunities that we want to explore! The main focus at the moment is developing our coaching and mentoring practice, which will work nicely with growing our property portfolio and networking business with Progressive Property.

Education, training, learning

Always looking to learn new things, my next interest in the property area is commercial conversions. Outside of property, I'm about to start my NLP Master Practitioner and complete a coaching accreditation. Working as a project manager also means I'm constantly learning and adapting to new and different project management disciplines.

I'm also really interested in how our mind and bodies are connected, I am a qualified craniosacral practitioner and a strong believer in setting good and positive intentions to improve quality of life.

Favourite books

- Robert T. Kiyosaki, *Rich Dad Poor Dad*
- Mark Manson, *The Subtle Art of Not Giving A F*ck*
- Eckhart Tolle, *The Power of Now*
- Rhonda Byrne, *The Secret*

Contact details

Website: www.capstone-group.com

Email: sarah@tspiuk.com

Sarah's Answers

How do I choose the right education, training and learning for me?

Go to the free events offered. There are lots of free events that training companies will do. Then, network when you are in the network meetings, ask people what they have done, what works for them, but this is for information only. This is a bit like looking for a new school for your child, you kind of need to see how it feels. People can give their opinions, but until you are in that environment you are not going to know how it feels for you.

Do some research, attend as many free days as you can. See if you can compare the offers – what's on offer, what can you get for your money – and then just pick one.

What happens when I start learning and realise there's more I don't know than I do know, or that there's too much to learn?

Don't panic. Take it in bitesize chunks. It is 100% going to happen, and the quicker you understand that, the quicker you can get over it. If you don't hit the point of thinking, oh my goodness there is so much to know, then are you really paying attention in the first place?

How can I use my thoughts to help me do what I want?

It depends on what your thoughts are.

How do I know which people to connect with to help me?

Practice and networking. There are key people you will need to build relationships with to help you on your journey. Some of these will build your power team, which is made up of experts in the field, like estate agents, letting agents, solicitors, people that know about the strategy you are doing, brokers. You've got all the different people along the purchasing process. If you think about the interim process of buying a property, you will identify who can and who will help you.

You'll need to build relationships with all of those people over time but, depending on where you are on your journey, you will have different needs at different times. Stay connected, make the most of your network, do regular 1-2-1s and the answer will start to come to you rather than you having to find it.

Is free help real help for me?

Of course, as long as they aren't trying to get you to sign up for anything.

How shall I prepare for opportunities?

Do your research; understand what opportunity there is in the local area. Look at websites out there such as Mouseprice. Look at property prices, assuming this is an opportunity for a property, but for an opportunity to work with someone or take on a new training course I think the same thing applies.

Which beginners' property books would you recommend?

Again, I think I will just go back to *Rich Dad Poor Dad*, because it's great around the whole ethos of it all. Also, any of the Rob Moore books and there are plenty of them. Perhaps look for a property book bundle deal on Amazon somewhere.

Which property strategy should I follow?

That completely depends on your interest and what you are trying to achieve. So, if you want a high cashflow, you might look at HMO or serviced accommodation, but that also comes with more risk. Or if you are looking at growth strategies you might want to make your money, go further and buy multiple properties that you don't get a lot of yield out but are in a high growth area. So, it really comes back to what are you trying to achieve.

How do I get the properties I want?

- Determination
- Understanding what it is you want, where it is
- Planning

Most things are achievable – you just need to know how to overcome your challenges.

What kind of money do I need to get my first property?

Again, this depends on the property, the size of the deal. The basics are you will need deposit money and you will most likely need refurb money. You should do, otherwise you're probably not buying a very good investment. You will need stamp duty and you will need a few thousand put aside for fees.

How can I find people I can trust to give me the right guidance?

By speaking to as many people as you can and trusting your judgement. Also, research. You can research companies to see if they are training outfits or people trying to get you to part with money. There are lots of reviews out there and you can look at them on social media. If it's more of a personal relationship you are developing, it's the same as any other relationship – you need to allow time for it to build.

45. Sharon Griffiths

About Sharon

Sharon started to learn how to invest in property in 2017 and has built up a buy-to-let portfolio with her husband which, along with her pension, has enabled her to fund her chosen lifestyle. She is a Director of The World Game Changers CIC and is a published author, trained life coach and experienced educational professional, having worked in the educational sector for over 30 years in a range of roles, including teaching, training and management, while also raising her two daughters who were born in the late 1990s.

Based	Essex UK
Investment location	Stoke on Trent and south Essex UK
Strategies	Buy-to-let
Favourite sayings/ affirmations/mottos	• You can change your life • Identify, Commit, Execute, Receive, Review, Reiterate, Rest, Revitalise • I am unapologetically me • It's better to say I'm glad I did than I wish I had • When fully present, life changes • We are magical human beings and a thought is a powerful force when concentrated • Let it go • Love changes everything
Three key learnings you would like to share with readers	• When you know why you are doing something, the what and how will follow. • The solution is in the problem, but with a different way of thinking than what led you there. Curiosity and Creativity will help you find it. • Listen to yourself and trust yourself. You are the person that knows what you desire more than anyone else.

Age 61

Job (if in a job previously)

Educational professional and advocate.

Why did you leave your job?

I needed to change my life, because I wasn't quite where I wanted to be.

What do you love about your life now?

I can live my highest values, choosing, scheduling and creating the future with and for those I love. I can go to bed when I want and wake up when my body chooses.

Education, Training, Learning?

- Experienced teacher and education curriculum manager, post-degree level
- Trained life coach, judo coach, risk assessor, advocate and reflexology and massage practitioner
- Property training, coaching and mentoring learning programmes with Progressive Property, Why Property Works, NC Real Estate
- Personal Development programmes including The Vee Coaching Method, New Insights Coaching, Super Genius, Millionaire Mindset Intensive training, Mindpower with Robin Banks, nine 12 Week Year masterminds
- Ongoing evaluation of learning and teaching since 1984

Favourite books

- Colin Turner, *Shooting the Monkey*
- Napoleon Hill, *Think and Grow Rich*
- Stuart Goldsmith, *The Midas Method*

Contact details

Website: www.sharongriffiths.com

Email: connect@sharongriffiths.com

Sharon's Answers

How do I choose the right education, training and learning for me?

For me, it goes back to a question that I often ask myself: 'What do I really, really want and why?'. This is because if I know

- Why I want what I really, really want,
- What I enjoy
- What I like to do
- And what I'm curious about

I can then focus on finding out about that particular subject or reason that inspires me or gets me going. So, maybe if you're starting out and you don't have a clue what you are doing, these could be good questions to start with. You can then research who can help you; there is a lot of free stuff out there and you can just google questions about what you are interested in. Once you find the thing you are interested in, you can then begin the prospecting process. A good general book to help you is Simon Sinek's *Start with Why*.

What happens when I start learning and realise there's more I don't know than I do know, or that there's too much to learn?

What a fantastic place to be in. You suddenly hit a point when you think, 'Oh dear!' This is normal when learning new things. In my 30 plus years of working in the education sector, I've been asked this question numerous times and I also used to ask it, and not just in property learning. When somebody has reached that point, it's time to take a step back.

You've had so much stuff going into your brain, it's time to take a little rest and just begin to try out a bit of what you want to do, or just say 'What next?' and sleep on it or take a holiday.

Then you can begin to narrow down what you really want to do; you're sifting through all those things in the sweet shop to find out what sweets you like so you can head towards them. A good general book to help you identify the things to focus on that you want to learn about is Gary Kellar's *The One Thing*.

How can I use my thoughts to help me do what I want?

Your thoughts are very powerful forces when concentrated. So, with that knowledge and awareness, you can do anything you want to with them. You can think, 'Right, what do I want? Ok I want that. Right, how do we do that?' And you can think, 'I want to go shopping; I want to buy property' or any thoughts you choose. Just pick something, use your chosen thoughts and direct each one towards where you want to be.

Once you've got that end point in your mind, you can then use your thoughts to create the actions you want to implement, to achieve what you want to achieve. Create from your thoughts, entertain that thought and take it to where you want to be. A great book that is helpful for this question is *Mindpower into the 21st Century* by John Kehoe.

How do I know which people to connect with to help me?

This depends on what you want help with really. If you know what you want help with, you can go searching for those people. And when you search, something within you will guide you to where you want to be and relevant people will appear – I have learned and experienced this myself. When you focus, this will be a filter to enable you to deflect anyone that doesn't help you, and you will allow in that space only things and people that will help.

You will know if you connect with somebody because you will feel it. It's as though they are on your wavelength.

Is free help real help for me?

Yes, absolutely. What is important here is to understand why the person is giving you free help. Sometimes people don't give the help for money, but they get something else in return. I have done this for decades, because I was helped on many occasions. I love to give free help. There is a fair exchange, but there comes a point where free help just fills your brain with stuff and then you get overwhelmed and don't know what to do next. So, to a point, yes, it's helpful for you.

How shall I prepare for opportunities?

Well, an opportunity is something that appears serendipitously or quicker than expected. It enables some form of good fortune to happen, so if you can't see what you are looking for, you won't recognise it.

A bit like a bus, an opportunity can come and go, and then it's gone. If you know what you really want and what you are doing, you're focusing your energy and actions on what you want to achieve, and suddenly you start to spot opportunities. What's that saying? 'If you fail to prepare, you prepare to fail.' So, it's not a case of preparing for opportunities, it's preparing and being primed for what you want to do and, in that process, you will spot the opportunities.

Which beginners' property books would you recommend?

The six I would start with are,

- Hazel De Kloe, *Why Property Works*
- Rob Moore and Mark Homer, *The 44 Most Closely Guarded Property Secrets*
- Rick Gannon, *House Arrest*
- John Foster, *Right First Time Property Investing the Trilith Way*
- Simon Zutshi, *Property Magic*
- Kevin McDonnell, *No Money Down*

If you are into serviced accommodation or furnished holiday lets, there is a good book by Kevin Poneskis called *Serviced Accommodation Success.*

We might as well stick a couple of mindset book in there, too, because when you invest in property you want to make money, and these three books help with this,

- Napoleon Hill, *Think and Grow Rich*
- T. Harv Eker, *Secrets of the Millionaire Mind*
- Robert T. Kiyosaki, *Rich Dad Poor Dad*

Which property strategy should I follow?

That depends on what you want to achieve. Let's clarify what a strategy is first. It's an overall plan. It's a bit like a football game, the overall plan is to win the game and win your game. You can put in lots of tactics to do this. From experience, I have learned that first of all, you need to work out what you want to achieve by the end of it, and why. then you can work out your plan.

Your strategy should be the one that will give you what you want to achieve in your life, and I can't tell you what that is because only you know the answer to that. But if you don't know what you want to achieve in life, maybe even before property you need to go back to identifying what you really, really want to do and spend your life doing.

How do I get the properties I want?

This depends what you want and why, because if you know what properties you want and what you want them to do for you, you can then go and find them. You will find a way to get them. So, for me, as a simple example, at the start I just wanted a little two-bed terrace that would enable me to achieve my life strategy and goals. I wanted to provide affordable houses that people can feel at home in. So, I looked for properties that could be turned into nice homes and that would also pay me the rent to be in those properties and be happy doing that. So, it's about looking at the end goal and why you want what you do

What kind of money do I need to get my first property?

You can use your own money or other people's money. With your own money it could be inheritance, pensions, a deposit you've saved for your first property; or you can work with other people who can lend you money, like angel investors that you pay back a certain amount, or you could work with family and friends.

If you know how much the property is that you want to get, all you need to find out is how much you need to get for it and then work out how you can get that. And that is building up capital either from yourselves or other people because it can be all of the property's value or it could be a small percentage.

How can I find people I can trust to give me the right guidance?

First of all, you need to know what you want them for. It's a very general question there. So, if you know what you want the people to give you guidance for, you can then begin to find out where they hang out. Go on a prospecting journey, then, whether it's online or in real life, go and speak to people. Get their recommendations and answers to your specific questions and then you can begin to narrow it down to who you can trust. Your gut instinct will help you along the way.

46. Shaz Nawaz

About Shaz

Shaz is a chartered accountant and Managing Director of aa chartered accountants. His firm specialises in working with property investors and his clients work with him because he is an active property developer. He has a significant property portfolio comprising mainly flats that have been converted from commercial to residential use.

Shaz has written several books and the most relevant to property investors is *The Property Investors' Tax Guide*. He also runs a tax course for property investors and speaks at property events. Shaz hosts the podcast 'Wealth Made Simple', and has a YouTube channel and a Facebook group.

He is currently working on a £12m GDV site, building 49 new homes in Boston, Lincs. His next site is a commercial conversion consisting of a mixed -use development with 21 new flats and commercial space.

Based	Peterborough
Investment location	Cambridgeshire and Lincolnshire
Strategies	Commercial-to-residential conversions and new builds
Favourite sayings/ affirmations/mottos	• You never achieve beyond your expectations • Don't wish it were easy, wish you were better • Success leaves clues
Three key learnings you would like to share with readers	• Do your research and make sure it's thorough • If it's too good to be true, then it probably isn't true – don't get caught up in the excitement and always be careful and considerate • You've got one life – take the opportunities you get, regret is an awful thing to live with

Age 44

Job (if in a job previously)

Investment accountant for JP Morgan.

Why did you leave your job?

Commuting to London was taking its toll and I always wanted to start a business, so I thought no better time than now (back in 2003).

What do you love about your life now?

Every client is different so that makes my job very interesting. I get to make a tangible difference to people's lives through training, mentoring, tax and business advice. It's my dream job.

Education, training, learning?

- Too much to list here but I'll add a few:
- Degree in accountancy and a Masters in Banking and Economics

THE 1ST PLACE.

- Member of Institute of Chartered Accountants
- Property training on a number of different strategies

Favourite books

- Jim Collins, *Good to Great*
- Robert T. Kiyosaki, *Rich Dad Poor Dad*
- Napoleon Hill, *Think and Grow Rich*
- Michael E. Gerber, *E-Myth Revisited*

Contact details

Website: www.entrustpropertytax.co.uk/home

Email: shaz@aa-accountants.co.uk

Shaz's Answers

How do I choose the right education, training and learning for me?

The best training and learning comes through taking action and doing. Nothings beats learning on the job. To decide on what is right for you depends on what you are looking for. You should make certain the training is relevant to what you want to learn. You should also make sure you are satisfied with the mode of teaching. If you like in-person events then online may not be right for you, and vice versa.

Also, think about how you best learn, so if you are somebody who likes reading then obviously books are going to be the right method for you, whereas if you're more of a visual person and like watching videos then a regular seminar might be best for you.

Regarding property training, obviously that's a personal choice, but from my point of view, I would say Progressive Property, because I've done lots of training with them and I'm also a trainer there. I think any course with them usually is fantastic value.

What happens when I start learning and realise there's more I don't know than I do know, or that there's too much to learn?

When that happens you're in the right place. We're all lifelong learners, so by the time we die we're only going to know a fraction of what we could have learned – nobody is ever going to be perfect and know everything that they need to know. No matter how experienced you are, every day is a school day and I think everybody should see it like that.

How can I use my thoughts to help me do what I want?

The first objective is to have clarity. I spend a lot of time thinking about what I want and what I am looking to achieve. I regularly review and amend my ideas until I feel certain they reflect what I want. After that, I set a detailed plan and roadmap to achieving the objectives.

In terms of using my thoughts to help me do what I want, I have programmed my mind to think positive and for my subconscious to feed positive thoughts. It's a bit like building muscle memory. I cut out all the negative stuff the best I can. I also find visualising helpful.

I run through everything in my mind every morning and evening. This repetition helps me enforce what I am looking to achieve. It sounds a bit woo but it works for me.

How do I know which people to connect with to help me?

Well, that's partly going on, let's say, social media and looking at the different influencers and people out there who are sharing information. Look for people you connect with, whose style works for you and whose information you've enjoyed consuming. Secondly, ask family and friends, and other people in the world of property who they've followed, worked with, like, and then check the map and see the ones that you feel comfortable with.

Is free help real help for me?

Free help is real help because most of us will get a feel-good factor with helping other people and if you don't have access to cash then you've got to start somewhere and start with everything that's out there that's free. But it's only going to get you started – if you want to make real good progress then you're going to obviously have to get some paid help, but free help is a good starting point.

How shall I prepare for opportunities?

By having a very open mind, by understanding you don't know everything, by understanding that there are people out there who can help you. I believe God helps those who help themselves, therefore be ready to take action, be ready to be uncomfortable and be ready for success.

Which beginners' property books would you recommend?

There are quite a few. *Property Investing Secrets* by Rob Moore and Mark Homer is a good one, and *Property Magic* by Simon Zutshi.

Which property strategy should I follow?

That's like asking me what I shall have for lunch, or what car should I buy next. I've no idea whatsoever and it's about people figuring out what they really want to achieve from their property business. So, it's difficult for me to sit here and give people a blanket answer but what I would say is

- Go out there and learn about the different property strategies.
- Figure out what you want to achieve and then work out which strategy is going to be the best to help you do this.
- BUT choose a property strategy that excites you, that you can see yourself doing for the next 5, 10, 15 years. If you can see yourself doing for 5, 10, 15 years then that means you're excited about it, and you're more likely to be successful doing it.

How do I get the properties I want?

By going out there and making offers for them and making sure they stack up. Simple as that.

What kind of money do I need to get my first property?

If you can use No Money Down and Other People's Money, you don't need any money whatsoever. In reality, however, you'll need some money, because you need to invest it in yourself and learn how things work, but generally to buy a property you need no money whatsoever. For example, right now, I'm buying properties that are joint ventures with other people and I'm not using any of my cash. So, in reality you need no money as long as you've got the resources and access to people who have the money.

How can I find people I can trust to give me the right guidance?

Ask other people that you trust for recommendations – people they know, like and trust –and use their experience. Then work with those people and, importantly, talk to them, test them out, make sure that you get a warm cosy feeling by talking to them and then try them out. Some will work, some won't work.

47. Stephanie Taylor

About Stephanie Taylor

Stephanie Taylor is a property investor, Co-Founder of award-winning property management and development company, HMO Heaven, and Co-Founder of Rent 2 Rent Success which has inspired thousands of none-traditional investors to get started in property. Along with sister and business partner Nicky, she bought a multi-million-pound portfolio of multi-unit blocks, commercial property and HMOs in her forties.

Voted Inspirational Person of the Year 2021, Stephanie has been featured on the BBC, Entrepreneur, Business Insider and The Telegraph. She is author of the number 1 best-selling book Rent 2 Rent Success; host of The Rent 2 Rent Success Podcast and a passionate advocate that ethical property investment is open to everyone.

Based	Newport, South Wales
Investment location	Newport, South Wales
Strategies	Commercial to residential conversions, multi-unit blocks, HMOs, rent-to-rent
Favourite sayings/ affirmations/mottos	• Believe bigger • Be bolder • Be a gamechanger

Job (if in a job previously)

Project Management in financial services.

Why did you leave your job?

I would have stayed in financial services, contracting until retirement, had it not been for one phone call. I know I wouldn't have had the courage to try property if it hadn't been for the call that changed everything; the everyday happening that changed my world.

My mum telephoned me one sunny morning while I was getting ready for work in my beautiful harbourside flat in Bristol. Getting ready for the onslaught that was life at the bank. Mum didn't call me in the mornings. She rarely asks for anything, and that's why I should have taken it more seriously.

Mum was ill. She tried to sound upbeat, but I could hear that she was scared. She called because she needed the reassurance we all need when we feel sick and anxious and afraid. I feel so ashamed because I was worried while we were on the phone. Yes, I was worried about Mum, but I was also worried about work. I was worried about being on time, and the project meeting, and the presentation, and, and, and... and so many other things that seemed so important at the time.

That was the day something changed for me. As I sat at my desk that afternoon, it hit me like a punch in the belly. It was the moment that I let myself see what my heart already knew. My mum was scared and alone in Birmingham and I still went to work in Bristol. I should have been with my mum – nothing was more important than that. Not the projects or the meetings or the deadlines or the presentations.

It came to me with clarity that day that the bank would be absolutely fine without me, but my mum wouldn't be. Do the things we insist are so important actually mean anything to us and our lives? I'll bet there are very few people who, on their death beds, wish they'd spent more time working at a bank.

And there are countless millions of people all over the world who wish they'd realised sooner how to create the freedom to live a life they really want, with more time for their loved ones.

What hit me that day was that I wanted to be able to choose to prioritise my life and focus on the people and things that mattered to me the most. That's when I knew that I had to make flexibility my reality. I needed more freedom. I wanted a passion and a vision and a proper life, not just a job. That day, I made making the leap a must, and I finally committed to feeling the fear and doing it anyway, and to working out how to get started in property with little money.

What do you love about your life now?

I love that I'm living a life I didn't even know was possible for people like me. I was a teenage mum on benefits at 18, and I found it difficult to imagine owning my own home, never mind owning a portfolio of properties. It blows my mind that our property businesses generate more income in a month than I made in an entire year as a contractor in demanding full-time roles.

Three things that I would like to share are too big to fit in the box above, so here they are. These are things that really light me up:

- Sharing what I've learned with my adult son Alex. Now he's creating financial freedom for himself. After bringing him up in the context of scarcity and having the feeling I was letting him down in terms of material things I could provide, I'm now able to show him how to create value and abundance for himself, his family (if he chooses to have one) and beyond. Alex is now saving and investing, and has bought his first property with a long-term plan for the future.

- With my sister Nicky, I'm setting up an accommodation and education trust to help young adults. I remember my struggle to get a decent home. I still recall clearly, walking into a lettings office, the lady looking up from behind her counter, looking at me and saying, 'we don't have anything for people like you'. And it's such a joy to know we are helping others who may struggle to find beautiful, affordable homes they love. The trust we create will provide education as well as accommodation so the young people understand how to create their own wealth and can continue the giving cycle.

- My third joy is sharing the message with other people that there is an ethical way to get started in property with little money. It's a joy to inspire people who have never thought property investment was possible for someone from their social, economic or ethnic background to know what is possible and to do it. Each time I see our students leaving their jobs because of the income they're creating through property, it is a joy.

Education, training, learning?

- A range of education, training and learning courses by providers that focuses on rent-to-rent training

- Various personal development courses

Favourite books

- Brooke Castillo, *What's Possible*
- Rachel Rogers, *We Should All Be Millionaires*
- Jeff Olson, *The Slight Edge*

Contact details

Websites: hmoheaven.co.uk; blowupyourlife.com; rent2rentsucess.com

Linktree: https://rent2rentsuccess.com/links

Email: hello@hmoheaven.co.uk

Stephanie's Answers

How do I choose the right education, training and learning for me?

I think it's really important to spend some time working out

- what it is you want and
- what result you want to achieve from that learning

And then go into the training, not waiting for anyone to give it to you, but determining that you're going to take the training and create the result that you're looking for.

What happens when I start learning and realise there's more I don't know than I do know, or that there's too much to learn?

These are both thoughts and it just comes from your brain being fearful because it doesn't like not understanding things. It doesn't like not knowing things, it feels dangerous. Expect to feel like that sometimes and just start taking the steps one at a time. Everything you can now do, from reading to driving, at one time felt like a lot to learn. There are people doing this, so you can do this too. When I get in the car of a learning situation, I make sure to put myself in the driver's seat to get the result I want. Don't be a passive learner. Be active to create the result you want.

How can I use my thoughts to help me do what I want?

Most of us operate from our unconscious thoughts most of the time. If you notice that the results you're creating in any area of your life are not the results you want, it's likely that your unconscious thoughts are not supporting your conscious ones. That's why it sometimes feels like you have an angel on one shoulder and a devil on the other.

We can begin by noticing when unhelpful thoughts come up. I remember, I had a thought that 'business isn't for me', which was creating that result in my life. Sometimes we can't move immediately to 'business is for me', but we can use bridge thoughts such as 'it's possible' and 'maybe I can do this too'. These thoughts drive the right kind of feelings that we want to achieve success.

So, you can use your thoughts to help you, by choosing a thought that you can actually believe right now and practice believing it. It is a practice. Every time we do something for the first time, we have to believe in something we don't have evidence for yet. It's so worth developing this practice because when your subconscious mind and your conscious mind are in alignment, things become easier.

How do I know which people to connect with to help me?

I think it's important to look at the people who've got the results that you want and the people whose values align with your own.

Is free help real help for me?

Well, it can be. Some people do give their time freely and you'll find a lot of information that's going to help you, especially at the beginning with understanding the pros and cons of a particular strategy. You can take the free help and assess after that whether you have enough or need more help.

How shall I prepare for opportunities?

Be ready and know what you want, because when you know what you're looking for you're more likely to see it.

We've all heard that, for example, when you are buying a specific make of car suddenly you start to see them everywhere – it's not that there are more of them, but now you can see more of them because you're focused on them. And it's the same with opportunities.

When we started looking for a property to buy, suddenly, we could see them everywhere.

When we were looking for a commercial property, when we were looking for rent-to-rent properties, when we were looking for properties to buy, suddenly your eyes are open to those opportunities.

So, how to be ready for an opportunity is to know what you want, and to have taken the first steps that enable you to take the next step to the opportunity. Sometimes, that can be finding information; sometimes it can be putting your credit record straight. These are the small steps that mean you can say yes to opportunity when you see it.

Which beginners' property books would you recommend?

My own book, which is called *Rent 2 Rent Success* and it's all about the ethical way to get started in property without buying it.

Which property strategy should I follow?

The one that gets you the results you want. So, I think it's really important to think about

- How much money have I got?
- How much time have I got?
- How much knowledge have I got?
- What do I want to create in my life – do I want assets that I don't need to invest very much time in OR do I want to work to get the maximum cash flow on those properties?

So, I really think it's a case of answering those questions first and then that will determine which strategies are the best for you.

How do I get the properties I want?

Look for them. Part of that is looking on the online portals but also you can look for properties by going direct to property owners, estate agents, property sourcers and your wider network. Let people know what you're looking for so that they can bring opportunities to you.

There are also ways of looking into probate properties through connecting with probate professionals. It's really networking within the community that you're in so that properties begin to come to you.

What kind of money do I need to get my first property?

Well, it depends on how much the property costs. Usually, it's 30% of the property value you need for buying cost, but you also need another 5–10% for purchasing costs and then you may need money for refurbishment. You can use your own money or private finance, or crowd funding or more formal finance; you might use development finance. There are lots of different ways to be able to attract funds to you that you need for a property deal.

How can I find people I can trust to give me the right guidance?

Be clear on what you want

- The type of strategy you want to do
- The values of the people you want to work with
- The type of support you want
- The kind of mentorship you need and then look for people who are offering that.

48. Tony Harding

About Tony

I started as an estate agent through the early 90s' recession. I then moved away from property and spent over 10 years as an IT Business Manager until I had an opportunity to own 50% of a scaffolding company. Alongside the scaffolding, I managed a property maintenance and construction company working on public sector projects. Then I had that lightbulb moment where I wanted to come full circle and get back to property and I couldn't be happier.

In the last few years we have built an HMO portfolio worth £1.5 Million with a monthly rent role of £13k per month. In the same time, we have sold property of just over £1 million with profit of £400k.

Based	Brentwood, Essex
Investment location	Essex and Stoke-on-Trent
Strategies	HMOs, Flips & Commercial Conversions
Favourite sayings/ affirmations/mottos	• Don't waste time on the things you can't change, focus on the things you can for the better. • • Be positive, believe you can.
Three key learnings you would like to share with readers	• I believe you can never know everything so always be ready to listen to other people. You can learn from their experiences and can always learn more. • If you want to succeed you need to have focus. It is so easy to let life drag you off in different directions and this may well slow your progress as it has for us when having another child whilst renovating our home. When life takes you away from the path refocus and go again and you will get back on track and see the results. • When you are learning from the help given to you by others remember the steps up the ladder and when you are where you want to be, give back and help others.

Age 49

Job (if in a job previously)

I have spent over 15 years in the construction industry. Before that I was an estate agent for 6 years, and I provide health and safety advice to small businesses.

Why did you leave your job?

I looked at my life, the amount of hours I was working and the fact I had three young boys, and just knew I wanted more freedom. I wanted more quality time with my wife and children and the financial freedom to live how we wanted to live.

What do you love about your life now?

I get to spend time with my boys in the morning before school and I am there most days when they get home. I get to see them do football, rugby, boxing, karate or whatever else they are up to. I love that my wife Sarah and I are doing this together and looking at how we can focus purely on our business and our family.

Education, training, learning

As well as all of the property training that we have done and continue to do, we are focusing on self-development for our property training and mentoring. This includes becoming NLP Practitioners and gaining an ACCT Coaching accreditation. I also have various qualifications with NEBOSH and CITB which enables me to ensure health and safety is up to standard on our sites.

Favourite books

- Robert T. Kiyosaki, *Rich Dad Poor Dad* – this was a game changer for me
- Mark Manson, *The Subtle Art of Not Giving A F*ck* – a refreshing view
- Eckhart Tolle, *The Power of Now* – makes you focus on what's important

Contact details

Website: www.capstone-group.co.uk

Email: tony@tspiuk.com

Tony's Answers

How do I choose the right education, training and learning for me?

There are a number of companies out there that are offering training, some of them are better than others. I have only done training with Progressive Property, so I can only judge by the training I have had, but I would look at one of the courses that offer you a broad view on all of the different strategies because until you have done all of those different strategies you are not going to know what is most likely to fit with what you are looking to achieve.

I would go on a course that offers a Mastermind or Masterclass course – usually a 3- or 4-day course – which gives a little bit on every single strategy and that just gives you a much broader view of what type of things you can do to make money in property. I think that is a great starting point for anyone.

What happens when I start learning and realise there's more I don't know than I do know, or that there's too much to learn?

Don't put too much pressure on yourself because you can't know everything and you're never going to know everything – even if you are in this business for 20 years you won't know everything. So, just take a step back, look at what is important for what you are actually doing and learn as much as you can about that and the rest will come later. You don't need to know everything to be successful.

How can I use my thoughts to help me do what I want?

Everyone is different on that. I tend to sit down and bounce ideas off my wife or my friends, or other people in the industry. If you have something new you want to do that is in your mind and you think it's possible, then talk about it. Your thoughts are important but sometimes you're full of good ideas and sometimes not so good ideas, so getting other peoples' opinions is a good one.

How do I know which people to connect with to help me?

There are a lot of people in this industry. In the property world there are so many people willing to help but there are also some shady characters out there as well. In my experience, there are a lot more good people than there are bad but, at the same time, all I can say is go out talk to lots of people, try and get to know them. This is the best way to find out if your values are the same, if you feel good about that person, if they respect you. It's very much a personal thing trying to judge people.

Is free help real help for me?

I would say it is in many cases. There are a lot of good people out there and a lot of people will help you and not expect anything in return. When you are talking about training and mentoring, you've got to weigh up the balance of what you are paying and what you think you are getting for you money. But there are people that will help for nothing and will share their experiences with you, talk to you about what they are doing and point you in the direction and, yes, it can be free and can be very helpful.

How shall I prepare for opportunities?

Preparing means having a good team around you. Even if you haven't bought any properties yet, I would start talking to various different solicitors and contractors. I would start building relationships and getting to know people.

So, when you have got a property, when you do find the deal you want to go ahead with, you already have your solicitor in place. If you put an offer in and it's accepted, the first thing the estate agent is going to say is can I have your solicitor details. That's not the time to then go and start finding the right person so start talking to people now, getting to know the people that you think you're going to work with, and then you are good to go when you find something.

Which beginners' property books would you recommend?

There are so many out there – the Rob Moore books are very good, and there are other books on HMO. I would just have a look out there. I know Kevin McDonnell has an excellent book on No Money Down strategies. It just depends on what you are going to be doing. Look at books which are going to be best suited for what you are trying to achieve.

Which property strategy should I follow?

That's a big one. I would say, sit down and make a bit of a board up and work out:

- what money have I got?
- how much experience have I got?
- what am I trying to achieve in the short term?

So, you want to have your short-term goals and your long-term goals.

If you look at your short-term goals and what you are trying to achieve, that is going to lead you to your strategy. It's impossible for someone else to tell you what strategy's best for you because everyone is different. What area do you live in? How much time do you have available to you? What help have you got around you? There are so many variables to these questions. Sit down with someone and they might be able to point you in the right direction, once they have spoken to you about it, but I couldn't answer that without talking to the individual.

How do I get the properties I want?

Once you have decided on your area and your strategy then get to know that area as much as you can. Get to know the areas that are good/bad/have good infrastructure around them like bus routes, train routes, supermarkets, work areas.

All of those are so important and the better you know your area the better you will know if something is a good deal or not. You'll know if you are paying over the odds for it or, if it's a good area, you might pay a little more for it. It's all about the local knowledge and getting to know your area as much as possible.

What kind of money do I need to get my first property?

Again, there are so many variables in that. What area are you buying in? There are areas in the UK where you possibly need as little as £10–15,000 to get going. Some of the areas down south you're going to need close to £100,000 or more. So, it just depends on what area you are looking to buy in and what strategy you are doing.

How can I find people I can trust to give me the right guidance?

There are a lot of very good people out there. I invested in the Progressive Property mentoring programme. With the VIP programme at Progressive there were some mentors I got on very well with and some not so much. Everyone is different. You've just got to talk to people, have conversations and see who you get on with, because some could be very good or they just might not click with your personality.

There's a lot of knowledge out there and when you pick someone's brains you can tell the difference if someone knows what they are talking about it comes across in the conversation. So, talk to people, ask them questions, ask them about their experience and what knowledge they think they can give you. Talk to them as much as possible because the longer you are speaking with them, the better you are going to get a feel for the knowledge they have and whether your personalities are a good fit.

49. Victor Lupu

About Victor

Working since the age of 12, Victor has had more than 20 jobs, ranging from cleaning to project management, handling seven-figure businesses. He has studied, lived and worked in different European countries and business sectors, including the food industry, hospitality and property. He has a bachelor's degree in engineering, speaks several languages, and is a certified sports instructor. As well as property, Victor has a passion for nature, horses, being in the mountains, sports and cars. He is a strong believer in change and progress based on willpower, a good attitude, solid habits and strong relationships.

Based	Swindon
Investment location	UK
Strategies	Property development
Favourite sayings/ affirmations/mottos	• Anything is possible
Three key learnings you would like to share with readers	• Believe in yourself and your dream, focus on one thing at time. • Break everything into steps and progress every day. • Revise, strategies, recharge and keep going.

Age 32

Job (if in a job previously)

Property developer.

What do you love about your life now?

The possibilities, freedom and choice.

Education, training, learning?

- Progressive Property
- Paul Tinker Training Academies
- Mountbatten Estates mentorship – Property Development

Favourite books

- Napoleon Hill, *Think and Grow Rich*
- Dale Carnegie, *How to Win Friends and Influence People*
- Tony Robbins, *The Power Within*

Contact details

Website: www.wiserestates.co.uk

Email: victor@wiserestates.co.uk

Victor's Answers

How do I choose the right education, training and learning for me?

Everything is an individual decision so once you have doubled checked and it's in pace with what you're trying to get and what your goals are, I believe in a self-assessment way of deciding.

What happens when I start learning and realise there's more I don't know than I do know, or that there's too much to learn?

There is not too much to learn, and there is always the situation of thinking that you don't know enough and there is a lot to know. The most important thing is try to start with small goals, one at a time, and take action from the beginning because everything else will come in time. You don't need to know everything when you start.

How can I use my thoughts to help me do what I want?

I would say it's very important that early in the morning when you wake up you have an intention. So, when you're looking to spend a couple of hours doing something – for example, in property – you need to know and have an intention about those hours so you're focusing on one thing at a time. If you are thinking about speaking with an investor or anything else you need to have that mindset ready and be focused about your goals.

How do I know which people to connect with to help me?

At the beginning, you have to connect with everyone and see who you feel a natural connection with; who you feel you can offer value to, and they offer value back to you.

Is free help real help for me?

Yes, I would say help can come in many ways and if it's free it's even better. You can always learn from anyone.

How shall I prepare for opportunities?

Every single time you're trying to set up a goal, think about the resources you need. When it comes to your own knowledge and how to assess that particular deal, just start to gather that information in advance.

Which beginners' property books would you recommend?

- Rob Moore, *Multiple Streams of Property Income*
- Kevin McDonnell, *No Money Down Property Investing*
- Simon Zutshi, *Property Magic*

Which property strategy should I follow?

For the beginning, just let's say get your feet wet. I would start with rent-to-rent, because you get to know a lot about the property world and you get to know about handling tenants, handling contracts, managing properties. Get in contact with people, it's going to help you a lot with you experience and relationships.

THE 1ST PLACE.

How do I get the properties I want?

You have to have a wide range of options. You need to start looking over those properties and have a lot of marketing in place. You need to spend a lot of time trying to narrow down all those possible deals. But it's pretty hard to find the perfect deal – you just need to spend a lot of time to try and narrow it down and find it.

What kind of money do I need to get my first property?

Depending on your goals, and depending on the area of investment, I would say at the beginning you would need a minimum of 5% deposit and some money for the legals. If your first property can be a residential one in your own name, then you can start building up some equity and then you can rent that out. If you need something slightly larger, you can start with 15% as a landlord but, then again, the interest might be a bit higher. So, I would say, depending on the area where you live in England, it might be £10,000 or it might be £20,000. Speaking particularly about Swindon, I would say the entry level to own a property is going to be about £15,000.

How can I find people I can trust to give me the right guidance?

Every single piece of information that comes to you has to be double checked and understood by yourself – you need to do your own due diligence about every single thing. This is extremely important; even when it comes to legal people, every single contract and every single thing that you're offering or signing – you need to understand those things. So, it's very hard to have a straight answer for this question but basically, it's about your understanding and taking your time to understand and acknowledge all these details.

50. Vito Ianelli

About Vito

I am 55-year-old married man of 31 years with 4 children. I have 25 years of real estate experience, having owned my own practice for 17 years. I have started a Serviced Accommodation (SA) business with my daughter Daniela as well as running a business transfer agency. I have won, lost, learnt and made many mistakes along the way. I am looking to build my SA management business and help as many landlords and investors get amazing tax benefits and a better return on their investment.

Based	Aylesbury
Investment location	Milton Keynes, Watford, London, Surrey
Strategies	Serviced Accommodation, Commercial Mixed purchases, BRR.
Favourite sayings/ affirmations/mottos	If you don't risk anything, you risk everything. The teacher will appear when the student is ready.
Three key learnings you would like to share with readers	• Surround yourself with positive like-minded people. • Always help someone without expecting anything in return. • Be regularly trained and mentored by someone who has walked the walk before you.

Job (if in a job previously)

Owned my own estate agency for 17 years prior to starting my Serviced Accommodation business and Business Transfer Agency.

Why did you leave your job?

I didn't leave, I just sold my business.

What do you love about your life now?

Having the freedom to build my property business.

Education, training, learning

Progressive Property Training including completing the SA Intensive, No Money Down, Commercial Conversion, BRR Masterclass and Deal Packaging courses. I am also a lifetime member of the Service Accommodation Mastermind.

Favourite Books

- Robert T. Kiyosaki, *Rich Dad Poor Dad*
- Napoleon Hill, *Outwitting the Devil*
- Brian P. Moran, *The 12 Week Year*

THE 1ST PLACE.

Contact details

Websites: www.vito@vitoiannelli.com/ www.propertyshoal.co.uk
Linktree: https://linktr.ee/vitoiannelli
Email: vito@vitoiannelli.com

Vito's Answers

How do I choose the right education, training and learning for me?

Educate yourself to find out about the different strategies that are available and then find out which one is most aligned with your passion and goals.

What happens when I start learning and realise there's more I don't know than I do know, or that there's too much to learn?

Take a step back, try and perfect what you have learned so far so you're clear and then move on to the next part of learning.

How can I use my thoughts to help me do what I want?

Use your thoughts by talking to others and knowing that you're on the right track, and also by finding out what their views are to see whether you're on the right track.

How do I know which people to connect with to help me?

I choose people that I like, I can trust and I know have helped others.

Is free help real help for me?

Yes, because it's a starter. It's a start to potential paid help that at least gets you started, and you have an idea.

How shall I prepare for opportunities?

I suppose it's about keeping an open mind.

Which beginners' property books would you recommend?

Like I mentioned before, *Rich Dad Poor Dad* I think gives you an ideal way into property, assets and liabilities, etc, and the Progressive books.

Which property strategy should I follow?

Property that sits with your end goal and what you feel comfortable doing.

How do I get the properties I want?

You get them through going direct to vendor, through estate agents, and through your network.

What kind of money do I need to get my first property?

There is no money down, you need zero.

How can I find people I can trust to give me the right guidance?

I think social media gives you a good insight into people and obviously by talking to other people who have used them, but it all goes back to trust – I think that if you like that person you talk to them, you trust them and see if other people have actually benefitted from them and you align with them, that's how I would find my mentors really.

FINAL WORDS

by Alex Sapala

Are you looking for financial and time freedom to live life on your terms? Have you tried a lot of different ventures or courses but simply haven't gotten to where you want to be? Perhaps you've been fed a lot of hype by perceived experts promising that you'll get rich, only to not be given the attention you need after purchasing that expensive course or mastermind?

You have a big dream and big reason why: perhaps it's security and a legacy for your loved ones after you've gone; that private life-saving medical treatment; the private education for your kids or simply that dream holiday you've always wanted but have never found a vehicle to take you there – until now. If that's you, then you've stumbled into *The 1st Place* you should be!

I was in exactly the same place back in early 2000s, and had I come across the wisdom packed into this book back then, I have no doubt that my journey would have been much quicker and smoother. This aim – to smooth the path for others – is the inspiration that has propelled myself and Sharon to bang together those years of property wisdom, experience, challenges and successes to give you the leverage and, frankly, an unfair advantage in your property journey.

In this Property Investing Beginner's Mastermind series, not only will you understand what it takes and what you need to get ahead, you'll also learn that while there are challenges along the way, if you take certain proven specific steps, your success is almost guaranteed – as it was for the 50 contributors to this book, who are among the best in the industry.

We all know that times are tough right now – pandemics, inflation, industrial action, you name it, all issues beyond your control. It is well-documented that times of crisis are also times of opportunity and it is those who are well-equipped with the right knowledge and information and, most importantly, an action plan who stand prepared to take advantage of those opportunities.

Property has been proven to be the vehicle responsible for making the highest number of the top wealthiest people in the world. In fact, it was Andrew Carnegie who highlighted that '90% of millionaires become so through owning property', and Robert Kiyosaki said 'Property investing, even on a very small scale, remains a tried and true means of building an individual's cash flow and wealth'. And it is for this reason that property investing is no longer a luxury reserved for the privileged few but a necessity you can't afford to miss or do without – like heating in your home in winter.

It is well-documented that the biggest shifts in wealth happen during times of crisis. In fact, according to the annual Credit Suisse Global Wealth Report (2021), the global wealth gap widened during the 2020 Covid pandemic, swelling the ranks of the world's millionaires by 5.2 million, as the rich cashed in on surging stock and house prices. The question then is, which side of the wealth divide will you choose to be? It's what you choose to learn and study and the actions you take that will determine that for you.

THE 1ST PLACE.

There's no better place than *The 1st Place* property mastermind series to give you the low-down on the good, the bad and the downright ugly of what it takes, what you need and, most importantly, the immense rewards waiting for you on the other side of the wealth building via the property world.

As entrepreneur and broadcaster Armstrong Williams says, 'One thing I tell everyone is – learn about property.' This book is *The 1st Place* on the path to your property success. Here's to turning your fortunes around as that's the one thing and one thing alone that's in your control – how you respond to a crisis and what action you take. Enjoy, learn to earn, be curious and seek understanding and growth. See you on the other side!

Alex

Glossary of terms

Throughout this book, several acronyms and abbreviations are used by some of the contributors. Here is a list of the most common.

B2S	Business-to-supplier
BRR	Buy, Refurbish, Refinance
BRS	Buy, Refurbish, Sell
CC	Commercial conversion
BTL	Buy-to-let (also often called 'single lets'; sometimes styled B2L)
FM	Facilities Management
GDV	Gross development value
HMO	Home of multiple occupancy
LPO	Lease purchase options
MSOPI	Multiple Streams of Property Income
PPN	Progressive Property Network
R2R	Rent-to-Rent
R2SA	Rent-to-Serviced accommodation
SA	Serviced accommodation
UHNWI	Ultra High Net Worth Individuals

Printed in Great Britain
by Amazon

22051890R00116